TENDER VOYEUR

TENDER VOYEUR

A BOOK-LENGTH POEM BY

DONALD PLATT

WITH CONTRIBUTIONS BY

TREVOR FAIRBROTHER

AND PUBLISHED BY

GRID BOOKS | BOSTON

ALSO BY DONALD PLATT

Swansdown
One Illuminated Letter of Being
Man Praying
Tornadoesque
Dirt Angels
My Father Says Grace
Cloud Atlas
Fresh Peaches, Fireworks, & Guns

GRID BOOKS
Boston, Massachusetts
grid-books.org

Printed in the United States

COVER: John Singer Sargent, *Male Nude Seen from Behind, Arm Raised Over Head*, c. 1890–1915. Charcoal on off-white laid paper, 24 5/16 × 19 inches. Harvard Art Museums / Fogg Museum, Gift of Francis Ormond. Photograph © President and Fellows of Harvard College, 1937.9.24.

ISBN: 9781946830395
LCCN: 2025932360

for Nicola D'Inverno, Thomas E. McKeller, & John Singer Sargent

for Trevor Fairbrother

Contents

Proem: *Apartment*

2019

They finished construction of this ultra-modern building
back in August,
and only a third of its apartments have been rented, so I have

my pick of floor
and view. In case I separate from Dana, I've put in an application
for Apartment 522.

It's on the top floor and looks out over the wide river that flows
through our small city
and divides it in half. Dana and I live on the west side. I would

be moving
to the east. I love the word "apartment." How it says what it means.
I would be living

apart from her. I love the apartment's huge, empty rooms.
I wouldn't want
to spoil that emptiness with furniture. Before I met her,

I never knew
black could have so many textures. Curly, black, lambswool jacket.
Black, flouncy, organdy

skirt. Necklace of garnets like gouts of blood strung on a gold chain
against her shiny
black silk blouse. I would bring to my apartment only a few choice things—

one futon, one
faux-Persian rug. No posters in chrome frames. Leave the walls white.
I'd luxuriate

in uncluttered space—eight hundred and fifty-four square feet of it
to be exact.
I would leave my life empty to make room to grieve

for my marriage
of thirty-one years, for the woman I love but find it hard
to live with.

This morning I dreamed that I walked across a pasture of browned-out
grass towards
a herd of horses trying to graze that scraggly verdure

they'd already
cropped down to the roots. One of the horses had two heads.
I reached out

to stroke the left head and found that its right side had wasted away
until it was only
bleached bones. I stroked those bones and tried to imagine the firm

flesh, muscles, warm
black-velvet skin that should have covered them. I felt only
the jawbone's

ridges, worn-down molars. Then the two-headed horse split apart
and became two
horses the size of Welsh corgis. The miniature horse with withered head

turned to me
and said its deformity was the result of the locoweed it had eaten.
I was amazed

it could speak well-formed English sentences. It said, "Please feed me!"
I woke
and knew then that the two-headed horse was our marriage breaking

apart. "Feed me
please!" The double-headed horse was my bisexuality that Dana
would rather I deny.

Tender Voyeur

2005–2007

I. Boxes

Yesterday, filling out
an anonymous survey at work, I checked off the appropriate boxes,
"Caucasian," "married,"

"age 46–61," "number of children: two," "income:
$50,000–$60,000,"
but stopped when I came to "sexual orientation." I could choose

among "heterosexual/straight,"
"gay/lesbian," "bisexual," and "transgendered" or "refuse
to answer." For the first time

in my forty-nine years, I checked the box that said "bisexual."
Though nobody would know
but a Scantron machine, it felt freeing to mark the box

I fit into.
But what does that one word mean? The dictionary says "sexually
attracted to both

men and women." How confusing. Whoever heard of a bisexual
bar? There are
gay bars, leather bars, topless bars, airport bars, and even neighborhood

bars, but not one
bisexual bar. That's my new profession—daytime bartender
at the Lonestar Bisexual Bar!

Business is slow. I look in the mirror and wink at myself.
Myself winks back.
I don't want that double life. How to be a bisexual

man within
a monogamous marriage? Dana won't look at me, refuses to talk
about bisexuality.

II. Reclining Male Nude with Hands behind Head

To make his living, John Singer Sargent painted oil portraits
of high society
women in sheer-sleeved, décolleté evening dresses, holding opening

gardenias in their laps.
He drew the nude male models he loved in charcoal on off-white,
cream, gray, blue,

or blue-green rag paper and collected them into an album
of figure studies
he showed no one. They were all working-class men out of work.

They were supposed to be posing
for his Boston Public Library murals. In one study, Nicola D'Inverno,
Italian immigrant,

sprawls on cushions thrown on the studio floor with calloused
hands clasped under his head.
He has wavy dark brown hair, a trim mustache, thick eyebrows. His cock

lies flaccid above
testicles the size of apricots that hang from a green bending branch,
ready to be picked.

III. Dream House

Maybe if we don't mention it, bisexuality won't exist.
Where that awkward word
used to be, just a small black hole sucking in tables, rocking chair, throw rugs,

washing machine, our bed,
the hanging asparagus fern. What gets repressed rearranges the furniture
so I'm a blind man

stumbling against a couch that wasn't in the living room
yesterday. Everywhere
I walk, I bang into hutches, armchairs, footstools that have shifted

places. Even the rooms
have been reversed. I walk through the front door into the bathroom. Dana
parks the car in our bedroom.

We cook dinner in the attic. Every morning I wake to a new
floor plan. The house
keeps dreaming. Today the basement occupies the whole second floor.

Our two daughters play
hopscotch and jump rope on the roof, hang from the gutters, eavesdrop.
"Come down," I yell. "Now!"

IV. Partial View of a Standing Male Nude

Nicola was nineteen. Sargent hired him as a manservant.
He worked for the painter
twenty-five years, lived with him in London, accompanied him

to Mallorca, Corfu, Venice,
Seville, Tunisia, and the Canadian Rockies, brushed mud from his suits,
kept his cigar box

full. Were they lovers? No one knew. Betty Wertheimer, a patron,
once told her niece that Sargent
was "interested only in Venetian gondoliers." Cantankerous bachelor,

he painted a nude Egyptian
girl standing with her back to us, but twisting her torso so we see her face
and left breast in profile.

Her downcast, long-lashed eyes focus on her fingers braiding
dark brown hair.
Her ripe lips pout, are pursed in concentration. The thick braid hides

her nipple. She could almost
be a boy. Her small right buttock, muscles pulled taut from the torque
of holding that twisted pose,

casts a long diagonal shadow across her right inner thigh.
The first folio
in the album of figure studies shows a nude male model thrusting

his chest up and out
toward us. While the Egyptian girl is all tensile stillness, he
flings his right

shoulder and arm back, reaches with his left arm straight up
to let us gaze forever
at his shaven armpit, pale unsunned place I would lick

and kiss, salt scent
of sweat, taste and tang of brine, man smell. His body is all
motion, a shout,

one man hollering to another, hallelujah of navel. He has erect
acorn-like nipples.
His circumcised cock swings free. It's a bell's bronze clapper tolling,

calling all of us
to worship here. His balls loll loose and cool against inner thighs.
Kneel. Take them in hand

as if feeling for bruises, soft places on the undersides of black plums.
Make him groan.
Plucked chicken skin of scrotum. Though your mouth goes dry, you must chant

Blessed be he that cometh
in the name of the Lord and give thanks for his risen flesh. Take. Eat. This is
my body. Sargent has shaded

the empty space along the right side of his torso so the rib cage,
glinting with spring
sunlight from the open studio window, stands out. The top of the page

slices off half the model's face.
Only the downturned chin and silent blurred mouth remain.
The sketchbook's sheet

isn't large enough to hold the whole body, left arm upflung,
flexed right arm
stretching back and away from his side. His hands are mourning doves

that have flown beyond
the edge of the rag paper. Where will they light? How do their soft
gray breast feathers

feel against open palms? Carefully cup one startled bird
to feel its quick heartbeat,
piston driving the blood through a four-ounce compression engine.

V. Bare Back

Backs are beautiful.
In the color photograph on the front page of the *New York Times*
Travel section, a young man

without a shirt walks away from us along the weathered plank porch
of a gay resort
near the sand dunes of Lake Michigan. Five other young men

sit in orange, yellow, green,
or pink Adirondack chairs, chat, flirt, and admire his bare back.
The spine is a shallow furrow

his lover's fingers will trace, pressing the vertebrae like frets
along the neck of an electric
bass guitar. It's a music I've never learned to play.

I can only imagine
those notes, fingernails gliding up and down my spine's steel strings,
then digging in

to make me moan. I love the names of the muscles so well-defined
on this man's back—
trapezius, latissimus dorsi, deltoid fascia, iliac crest. There are

four stars tattooed
just under his neck. A serpent's tail curls around his left triceps.
Do he and his lover

bareback? In the morning sunlight that falls across the knotted boards
of the porch and turns them
golden, it's hard to imagine these six young men going to barebacking

parties, having to take
antiviral cocktails, being "bug chasers" or "gift givers." Before he met
Nicola, Sargent

was described by a sitter as "a frenzied bugger" who frequented
the male brothels
of Paris and Venice in the 1880s. Always discreet, he painted

one of Oscar Wilde's circle,
Walford Graham Robertson, painter, memoirist, art collector,
then twenty-eight,

in the year before Wilde's infamous trial. Robertson stands in his calf-length
black Chesterfield
with velvet collar, white ascot, right hand on cocked hip, fingers splayed

like spider legs,
left hand holding a jade-handled walking stick. His aging poodle
with a yellow bow in its hair,

who liked to nip Sargent at least once before letting him begin to paint,
is curled at Robertson's feet
and matches his gray pants. Red-gold hair, blue-green eyes, pale face,

he is thin as a knife's
honed edge, beautiful, effeminate, a dandy. He is the fin-de-siècle
version of those six

young men in their baggy cargo pants and brand-name sneakers
horsing around and joking
on that sunlit resort porch. The long overcoat and elongated

canvas, seven-and-a-half feet
by four, make Robertson appear even thinner. When he objected
to wearing a wool Chesterfield

in the heat of August, Sargent replied, "But the coat is the picture....
You must wear it!"
His sitter retorted, "Then I can't wear anything else!" He posed naked

under the overcoat.
In one of the album's figure studies, a nude male model stands
with his back turned three-quarters

toward us, one hand on hip, the other behind his head. Each back muscle
is carefully rendered
in charcoal so the drawing becomes sculptural. It makes me want

to reach into the page
and trace his flexed deltoid. His outthrust buttocks are sketched
in a few quick strokes.

The nub of one nipple is visible under the upraised
arm. It's a small
thorn. Sargent has given us the illusion of sunlight

playing across that flexed
shoulder by erasing the charcoal with a hunk of fresh French bread
torn from a crusted baguette.

It's the same sun that warms the tattooed back of the young man hurrying
to meet his lover in their
hotel room. They'll pull the curtains, fuck in the dark with their eyes open.

VI. Two Sisters

"I paint what I see…
I don't dig beneath the surface for things that don't appear before
my eyes," said Sargent.

It was what he hoped all his patrons would believe.
It wasn't why
by the late 1890s most of English and American

high society wanted
him to paint their portraits. They never knew what they'd get.
In his painting of Ena

and Betty Wertheimer, the two sisters in their twenties stand
in low-cut evening dresses,
proud of their ample, half-bare breasts, at home in their bodies.

Betty wears rust-red velvet,
has silk geraniums in her upswept black hair. She leans into her sister,
pale naked shoulder

to shoulder. Ena's right arm circles Betty's waist and disappears.
Her disembodied right hand
reaches forward palm up as if to cup Betty's full, red-velvet

breast. Ena's other hand
rests on the glistening round knob of a waist-high, robin's egg-blue,
porcelain Chinese vase's

lid, as if to say that all of sexuality's multiple
ambiguities—
from the Latin *ambigere*, meaning "to go round, wander

about, argue, drive
both ways"—are held fast in that Pandora's box, are not to be opened,
only hinted at.

Betty's elongated white right arm hangs down by her side,
follows the curve
of her hip. She holds an open transparent silk fan out toward us

so we see only one vertical
line, its gold-edged ridge head-on, the fan itself foreshortened
to a sliver of diaphanous

fabric through which her thin wrist wavers. It is a miracle
of perspective—once seen,
never forgotten. Betty's hazel eyes gaze straight into ours.

The Chinese vase
whose blue, gold, and rose hues shadow Ena's white satin dress
holds its bright secrets, glows.

VII. Triple Portrait with Rhododendrons, 1985

I once watched Jules, my bisexual girlfriend, make love to Kim,
her bull-dyke lover
who didn't know that Jules and I slept together. The three of us

were hiking through the Smokies'
rain and fog in June. We'd climbed into the clouds. The morning light
was egg-yolk golden

against the cream canvas of our tent as we woke slowly, kept dozing,
lay there, lazy,
basking in our body heat trapped in unzippered sleeping bags

of eiderdown rated
for midnights below zero. Jules turned on her side away from me
and started kissing

Kim, their tongues flicking, thrusting wetly into each other's impatient
mouths. "You can watch,"
said Kim, "but don't do anything." Jules worked her way down,

unbuttoning Kim's
lumberjack flannel shirt to lick her dark brown nipples until they rose
and glistened. Then Jules

moved lower, her tongue leaving its shining snail trail of saliva
from areola's dark aureole
against white freckled breast, past ribs, to navel and mons veneris where

a forest fire raged
among that golden pubic hair. Kim arched her back, bucked, moaned.
She raked her red nails

through Jules's black hair. Their twenty fingers were firefighters
that spread the blaze.
Nothing could extinguish their bodies, tensing, writhing, relaxing,

then catching fire
again. I had a hard-on. Strapped to that mast, hands tied behind
my back, I could only

listen to the fire roar around me like a siren's song and envy
their beautiful bodies'
pleasure, D-major scale that rose, fell, rose again to a soprano's

high note held
until all glass shattered, and then the kingdom come of orgasm
came and came.

Sweaty, they lay shipwrecked in each other's arms. I was jealous
and didn't want to share
Jules with anyone. The rage that filled me twenty years ago

is the same anger
my wife must feel when I mention men. Betrayal stuck in my throat
like a fine fishbone

I couldn't cough out. I left the two of them alone in that tent
and hiked half a mile
up the mountain. At four thousand feet the rhododendrons,

which had finished blooming
in the valley two months ago, were breaking into velvet blossom.
I walked backwards

from early summer into chill late spring as if I could recover
the love I'd lost that morning.
Wet with night rain, dark green leaves. Pink flowers opened all around me.

VIII. Tents

In 1916, in the middle
of the Great War, D'Inverno and Sargent hiked the Canadian Rockies
together with a guide

named Hastings, whom they hired at Lake Louise. Sargent wanted to paint
the two-hundred-forty-foot
Yoho Falls, which he first glimpsed on a postcard given him by a Boston

Brahmin. Sargent had turned
sixty. D'Inverno was forty-three, Hastings thirty. "It was raining or snowing,"
Sargent wrote his cousin Mary,

"my tent flooded, mushrooms sprouting in my boots, porcupines
taking shelter in my clothes,
canned food always fried in a black frying pan getting

on my nerves, and a fine
waterfall, which was the attraction to the place, pounding and thundering
all night." Sargent painted

the two streams of water hitting the rocks and sending up
an iridescent mist.
He also painted Hastings sitting on a stump, a brown wool sweater

draped over his shoulders,
his back to the campfire, where a black kettle boils, before their two
tents, white canvas

shining with early morning sun. Hastings has red-blond hair, the color
of sunlight on fallen
pine needles, a bushy mustache. He has just shaven his tan

lean face, but hasn't combed
his tangled hair. He holds something white in his large, strong hands.
Is it a potato he's peeling?

No, it's the plucked body of a young ruffed grouse he's shot and gutted
and will soon roast
on a stick whose bark he's stripped off with a jackknife. Its juices will bubble,

drip, and sizzle down
the spit's green wood. Was Nicola jealous of the younger man's
rough beauty? Of how

Sargent painted Hastings in oils, but only dashed off a quick
watercolor of Nicola
half-blurred by the campfire's smoke? Nicola took a photograph

of Sargent and Hastings
lying on a grassy hillside with bedrolls under their heads. They wear
brimmed hats and calf-high boots.

Sargent is smoking his usual cigar. Because they've been hiking all day,
Hastings has fallen asleep
with his arms crossed over his chest. From Nicola's angle it looks

as if Hastings rests his head
on Sargent's shoulder. The painter closes his eyes and listens
to the hum of honeybees

going from bull thistle, fireweed, goldenrod, goatsbeard,
to contorted lousewort,
purple fleabane, valerian, violet, buttercup, northern bedstraw,

red paintbrush.
"Now the weather has changed for the better," Sargent wrote Mary,
"and I am off again

to try the simple life (*ach pfui*) in tents on the top of another
valley, this time
with a gridiron instead of a frying pan and a perforated

India rubber mat
to stand on. It takes time to learn how to be really
happy." He painted

a watercolor of the tent where Hastings slept naked.
Crossed pine saplings lashed
together support the ridgepole. The tent is a white room

luminous with morning light's
gold leaf. The tent flaps are tied back so we see inside.
In one corner stand

the two halves of a fly-fishing rod whose tremulous tip will register
the brook trout's least
nibble, its hard strike, and then bend wildly like a dowser's wand

discovering well water
as the line runs through the reel between Hastings's raw hands.
Here's his tackle box

filled with hand-tied flies whose horsehair wings disguise the snelled
steel hook. Spread
on the damp ground, a red wool blanket beneath which Hastings

slept sound, while Sargent
listened all night to the waterfall. By the tent door, an enameled shaving bowl
spilling over with sunlight.

IX. Male Head in Profile

"I'm getting married," my beautiful student tells me, flushing proudly
from slender white neck
to freckled cheeks. Her brown hair is pulled back tight from her face.

Her blue eyes stare
clear into the future, ignite, and flash. "Congratulations!" I tell her.
What I can't say

is that marriage is a tumbling barrel that turns two rough-cut stones
end over end
against each other to grind, scrape, file, abrade, and wear them down

to smoothness so they
shine. It's taken Dana and me twenty years, two children, our daily
wranglings over household

chores, careers, work time, childcare, money for us to become
two polished rocks.
We're bands of red-brown quartz and opal, minerals compressed

into the soul's strata.
Agates. A contour map of forces greater than ourselves—
eons, temperatures

in excess of a thousand degrees Celsius, millions of pounds
of pressure per square inch.
The soul is an igneous, semiprecious stone. To stay in this marriage,

I've had to learn
that I love men and not to be ashamed of this desire.
Isn't the fault line

that runs straight through our marriage's bedrock
my love of men,
deep shifting of the earth's core that has taken me

forty-nine years to feel
and fully register? The heart is a broken seismograph.
Sargent drew

Nicola's profile in charcoal. Light glints off high cheekbones.
His matinée idol's eyes
are hooded. His nose is long and straight, "a noble Roman's nose,"

as my mother likes to say.
His angular chin sticks out. His mustache is soft and must tickle
like tufts of white, brown-speckled

feathers drawn across ribcage, sternum, nipples. His hair is black
and thick. He's twenty-two.
After Sargent's death, Nicola remembered posing for him

the first time. "He came
to the door himself, a big, burly, bearded six-footer, asked us
our names and directed me

to step inside and show my figure." It was winter. Nicola
shook the snow off
his blue peacoat and hung it on a chair. He unbuttoned his shirt,

pulled down his flannel pants,
and stood in a green thong in the middle of the room. He had
goose flesh. His nipples were

erect. The silence was tense with what went unspoken. "My brother
happened to be posing
for him that very day, and Mr. Sargent wanted to know

why he had not brought
me around before, because I was the 'very man' he wanted."
Sargent motioned Nicola

to stand next to the black, potbellied stove, threw more wood on,
and started sketching
him. He would sketch and paint Nicola for the next twenty-five years.

X. Cigars

D'Inverno boasted only
that he modeled for the Boston Public Library's *Freeze of the Prophets*.
When Sargent was commissioned

to paint Woodrow Wilson's portrait in 1917, Nicola recalled,
"I . . . actually posed
for Wilson's coat! Does that sound quite silly? I assure you

it was quite sensible
enough. By my posing for the coat part of the portrait the very busy
President was enabled

to shorten his sittings." The coat is black wool, double-breasted, fits
tight across Wilson's
chest, or is it Nicola's? The left hand hangs limply down

over the wooden scrollwork
of a leather armchair's armrest. Is that hand the widower President's?
Or the Italian immigrant's?

Is the hand weary or relaxed, heterosexual or gay?
It's rarely either . . . or.
The painting says it's both. Sargent drew Nicola in charcoal

for a whole year
before he asked him to be his valet. To make the long hours of posing
pass, they told each other

jokes. Sargent smoked cigars incessantly. His large pink right hand,
which held the flimsy stick
of charcoal, knew Nicola's every sinew, his lumbar triangle, each abdominal

oblique muscle.
"—Knock knock! —Who's there? —Lena! —Lena who? —Lean a little
closer and I'll tell you!"

That bad joke cracked Sargent up. They could be silly together.
"What's the difference
between a blue-throated macaw and a banjo? One

is loud, obnoxious,
and noisy. The other is a bird!" They both guffawed. When Nicola
went home, his clothes smelled

of Havana cigars. He liked the musky smell. So, when Sargent said,
              "I need a man
to draw my bath and generally run the house on Tite Street.

              I'll pay one hundred pounds…"
Nicola said yes. Dana proposed to me after we'd made love.
              We lay back winded

on the unmade bed, breathing in the reek of sex, the smell
              our bodies made together.
"Of course," I said. It was Christmas, two feet of snow. I took the garbage

              out to the curb, wearing only
Dana's red bathrobe. An old man, hobbling down the icy sidewalk,
              grinned. "So how the holidays treatin' you?"

XI. Male Nude Reclining on a Stairway

D'Inverno claimed that Sargent's "life was as orderly as that
              of a bishop. He was awakened
every morning at seven. His breakfast was on the table at the stroke

              of eight. After breakfast—
never before—his bath. Then, an hour with his correspondence,
              and at ten he was on the way

to the studio." He sketched Nicola stretched out nude on a cloth
              that poured like a mountain stream
down the wooden steps leading up to the mezzanine. Nicola pretended

              to sleep. It can't have been
comfortable. His body and the stairway make a diagonal
              across the page. Its center

is Nicola's uncircumcised cock, dark pubic hair against sunlit thighs,
              a calla lily's
golden pistil. A man's cock is no hothouse flower.

It's a bullfrog
risen from the swamp's slime to croak its guttural
desire over

and over, humid midsummer night's monotonous mantra—*Come here,*
come here!
It's an iron spike that loves the ten-pound sledgehammer that drives it

home into a creosoted
sleeper. No, cock is a cock is a cock, as Gertrude Stein
didn't say. It's a word

repeated by the mind's diamond needle stuck on a love song,
vinyl 78
that then keeps skipping, skipping on a hi-fi stereo, obsession's

endlessly revolving
turntable. It's a stuttering child's nursery rhyme, *Ride*
a cock horse

to Banbury Cross... Each stroke of Sargent's charcoal is a quick
caress, the love
he couldn't say, but which his hand spoke. So that Nicola

"might keep fit,"
Sargent paid for his classes at the Quiating Hogg Gym, where he learned
to box. Sparring, he would break

from a clinch, weave, feint, counterpunch—left jab, straight right, left hook,
a scoring uppercut.
"Occasionally, I wore a beautiful black eye, and whenever

this happened, I was certain
to be greeted by the master in the morning with 'Ah! I see
we have met another man

who is slightly the better.'" Because Nicola was raised in Clerkenwell,
London's Italian district,
and he'd started fighting at bantamweight, Sargent dubbed him

"the Clerkenwell Chicken."
He lifted weights, bulked up. He loved the thud his gloves made
against another man's

muscled ribcage, glistening with sweat that splattered with each punch.
He himself was often
black-and-blue. His nose got broken. Once, Sargent attended

a boxing tournament.
"It was my best night, and when I had put two men 'out'
Mr. Sargent quietly

left the club." The master had a temper too, threatened to thrash
a farmer who'd berated
him for riding his horse through a field of winter wheat. His favorite

curse was "Damn!"
He ordered a rubber stamp embossed with that word. "When things
went wrong," Nicola said,

"he would stamp everything in sight with his 'damn!' 'damn!' 'damn!'
'damn!'" Nicola's main job
was to "shoo away" from the door of No. 31 Tite Street

the lords, dukes, and marquises
who wanted to get their portraits painted. "I am exceedingly sorry, sir,
but Mr. Sargent is very

busy. Would you care to make an appointment?" What did the lords
think of a manservant
in morning coat and white ascot, black eye swollen nearly shut?

XII. The Chess Game

In Sargent's 1907 oil, two figures wearing harem
pants and flowing robes
lie on their sides on a grassy spit of land as big as a king-sized

bed that extends out
into a still millpond. The water reflects flecks of sunlight,
lavender-blue sky,

green leaves, shadows, white boulders of clouds, all swirled together
into the kaleidoscope
of sultry midsummer. It's hard to tell land from water. Here

everything shimmers, floats,
dissolves into pure color, into the pinky rhododendron red
of the nearest figure's

harem pants. Sargent loved fabric and has caught how the silk
glimmers, gleams
as it cascades over the full globes of Nicola's buttocks.

It's a waterfall of light
and shadow, each crease, pleat, and frothy fold of cloth suggesting
his firm flesh underneath.

Nicola wears a beige fez and has crossed his bare left foot
over his muscled bare
right calf. He stretches out his right arm in a fluent signature

of white silk sleeve
to move a black bishop on the checkered chessboard that is the center
of the painting. He plays

against a veiled man or woman in a lavender turban. He or she
rubs his or her chin,
considers her or his next move. We understand that the chess game

is a metaphor
for marriage, for the politics of sex and power between any two people.
The daily transactions

of men with men, women with men, men with women, women
with women are played out
on the black and white squares of the chessboard. I sacrifice my knight

and rook to take your queen.
If I pick up the kids at three o'clock, will you make love tomorrow
morning? How many

orgasms is the weekly grocery shop worth? If love's not on the shopping list,
along with two gallons
of milk, garlic, catfish, 60-watt light bulbs, and toilet paper,

it won't get purchased.
But love's no ledger where accounts receivable equal
accounts payable.

It's an afternoon spent in the presence of sunlight on stilled water.
Two people dress up in exotic
clothes from Constantinople, lie on the grass, play chess and make-

believe for the painter
who paints a place where pleasure ripples the millpond. He offers us
this lustrous leisure.

XIII. Madame X

Of course, no matter who the model, the veiled lady
with whom Nicola plays
the game of chess, whose lavender-shadowed shawl swirls and eddies

into a tidal pool
of silk spread out upon the grass, is Sargent himself. He's also
Madame X,

Madame Pierre Gautreau, née Virginie Avegno, Louisiana
beauty transplanted
to Paris, whose husband was a prosperous banker. Sargent

painted her
for the 1884 Salon and caused a scandal. She stands
clutching a black fan

and a few folds of her black evening dress in her left hand
whose fourth finger glints
gold with a wedding band. She tilts her left hip up and leans

her right thigh against
a round lacquered table so that its edge presses into her flesh.
She's bent her right arm back

to grasp the table's rim and twists her wrist at an awkward
angle. Her thumb juts
downward. Its crooked knuckle gets reflected in the polished table's

elongated ellipse.
She's swung her head away from the table so we see her face
in profile, upturned nose

resembling a ski jump, plucked eyebrows arched, small mouth.
The tendons in her neck
stand out. Her low-cut bodice's two black petals barely contain

her alabaster breasts.
One of its straps studded with brilliants has slipped off her shoulder,
cuts into her upper

right arm's plump flesh. She is sex incarnate, beauty, and disdain.
Like the nude Egyptian girl
that Sargent painted seven years later, she must wrench her body

to hold the pose.
Sargent loved to paint that theatrical tension, the body's brimming
sexuality about to break

free from culture's contortions. He knew its bit and bridle well.
He spent his life
posing, gay man as heterosexual bachelor. But each true painting

is a mask that also
reveals. Sargent told his critics, "I chronicle, I do
not judge." He painted

Madame X with all her makeup on. Her skin shines pearly blue,
    a dead woman's color.
He wrote his friend, the lesbian Vernon Lee, "Do you object

    to people who are *fardées*
to the extent of being a uniform lavender or blotting paper
    colour all over? If so

you would not care for my sitter. But she has the most beautiful lines
    and if the lavender
or chlorate-of-potash-lozenge colour be pretty in itself,

    I shall be more than pleased."
All Paris was shocked by his painted woman. On opening night, a friend
    exclaimed, "My, doesn't she look

decomposed?" Sargent, Mr. X, devised his own brand of makeup.
    To paint his wealthy patrons
he wore a white linen jacket, jaunty red carnation stuck

    in his buttonhole,
silk foulard tie, and dove-gray pants pressed that morning
    by Nicola's hot

coal iron. I wear a gold wedding band, write homoerotic
    poems that no editor
will publish because "they're overheated, excessive, and utter

    gibbering, adolescent
wet dream rubbish." Another editor even writes, "We must save you
    from yourself." Hard

blow job, I'd say. These poems are my album of figure studies,
    quick sketches of yearning
for some nameless man's strong quadriceps, his cramped calf muscles

    I would massage and run
my fingers along, skin downed with fine gold hair, up toward his hidden
    inner thigh. "He who desires

but acts not," wrote Blake, "breeds pestilence." Makeup can be
poison. Madame X's
chlorate of potash, her lavender skin powder, is now used

in insecticides.
Women who wore the lead-based cosmetics common in the nineteenth
century often developed

facial tremors or paralysis. Must beauty be toxic?
What happens
to desire when it's covered over with foundation

makeup? Madame Gautreau
took lovers. When she got old and beauty failed her, she became
a recluse, ordered the mirrors

to be taken down from her walls. Sargent lived with Nicola
as his manservant,
painted watercolors of the places where they went together

on vacation, Venetian
gondoliers poling tourists past the Bridge of Sighs, the dirty
green canal water

turned to azure sky. Is sublimation, art's wondrous
dangerous makeup
and make-believe, my only answer? Are poems only sighs?

XIV. Male Model Resting

I am too old for him,
this poetry-slam circuit rider who shouts his gay free verse
through bars in Boston,

beautiful man whose red-blond hair falls coyly across his freckled face
until he tucks the strands
behind his ear and looks at me with blue-black eyes that blaze

like lightning strikes
on rainless nights over hayfields waiting to go up in flames.
I want love's slash-and-burn,

but he treats me like the father I could be, my forty-nine years
to his twenty-two.
We sip hot chocolate at a kitchen table within earshot

of his mother who introduced
us. He's given me a chapbook of his poems. I am supposed
to be "encouraging."

I'm jealous of his poems, of their pain, of how easy gay sex
can be, collision of flesh
on flesh, one-night-stand fender-benders or three-way, freeway wrecks

from which no one walks away
unscathed. I want a love that "totals" me, but sex at fifty is always
complex. I cannot live

my heterosexual years over. I cannot be Verlaine
to his Rimbaud. I am
only stodgy "page verse" to his heart-in-your-mouth slam poetry.

Those blue-quartz eyes,
their color is quarried from clear, cold, spring-fed lakes, deep aquifers
that keep love's water table

full. I finish my hot chocolate, praise his good poems.
He will live the love
I cannot have. Sargent at my age sketched Nicola

in watercolors
resting on a bed. The walls are a wash of cool aquamarine.
Sunlight reflects off

torso and thighs so his body shines blindingly. He's closed
his eyes, head laid back
on a white pillow, left hand behind his head so we admire

his pumped-up biceps.
His right arm gathers the folds of red silk sheets and holds
the slippery gleaming fabric

against his white rib cage as if it were an armful of two dozen
long-stemmed roses
that Sargent has just given him for his birthday. In the background

the brown wooden stairs
up to the mezzanine parallel the diagonal of Nicola's torso.
Our bodies are a stairway

we climb slowly, languorously from one floor to another.
Nicola has drawn
his left leg toward him. His knee makes an upside-down V. A small

triangle of scarlet silk sheet
hides his genitals. The folds of drapery serve only to disclose
the bulge of his half-erect

penis. I remember waking early in a college dormitory.
My roommate slept naked.
It was hot. In his restless sleep he'd thrown the covers off.

First hesitant sunlight
fell across his thighs and showed me how his hard-on rose
from red-gold ringlets

of pubic hair. His cock was longer and thicker than mine.
Swollen
purple-red and orange-red, the shank's chafed skin was mapped

with big, blue, knotted veins
and the finer purple ones. I stared. I wanted to touch it. Two rocks
struck sparks within my loins.

XV. Sonnet Excerpted from an Index of First Lines in The Collected Poems of William Carlos Williams

So art thou broken in upon me,
    Apollo

So different, this man

so much depends

So this is death that I

So what the door was guarded

Soft as the bed in the earth

Solemnity of a bemused tiger,
    here in his eyes

Some leaves hang late, some fall

Somebody dies every four minutes

Sometimes I envy others, fear them

Sometimes the river

Sooner or later

Sorrow is my own yard

South wind / striking in—torn

XVI. Album of Figure Studies

                    I imagine Sargent opening
the black-cloth-and-cardboard covers of his album of figure studies,
                    crumbling leather spine,

watch him thumb again through the charcoal sketches of nude male models.
Over his shoulder, I see
how Nicola's hooded eyes, his long Roman nose, keep reappearing

among the models' half-averted
faces. Many of the drawings are of Nicola D'Inverno,
Nicholas of Winter,

his beautiful body changing over twenty-six years. The last
folio in the album
shows a young, lithe, lightly muscled man with his legs drawn up

under him, right wrist bent
and posed on his hip so the palm faces upward. His other arm,
perfectly perpendicular

to his torso and V-angled at the elbow, rests flat on an invisible
table of air.
Though Sargent made this collotype in 1921,

three years after
D'Inverno stopped working for him, the young man has Nicola's
thick eyebrows, soft shadow

of his mustache. Is it Sargent's memory of Nicola
at nineteen, dream boy
with a satyr's insatiable body? Fawn flesh still untouched,

he is Nicola
Di Primavera, Nicholas in spring. The drawing is an old
abandoned man's

dream of first love. Here is also Nicola D'Estate, his boxer's
lean, well-toned body
reclining on an unmade bed. He's pushing himself up

with his right forearm, right leg
dangling over the bed's edge, as if he's only now awakened,
after making love three times,

from a hot afternoon's sweaty nap. His long cock rests
on his white right thigh.
His left leg is raised on two silk pillows. He's Sargent's summer

lover. Here's also
Nicola D'Autumno, a man of forty leaning forward
on his left leg so only

the ball of his right foot touches the ground. He still has a boxer's
broad pectorals and thighs,
but his slim waist has thickened. Both arms are raised over his head

to form a Y,
a boxer's gesture to the yelling crowd after he's knocked
the other man out cold.

These charcoal sketches are Sargent's love poem to Nicola,
to the quarter century
they lived together. He collected the drawings he'd kept always

hidden in his studio's cupboards
and glued them to the album's pages so he would remember
Nicola. They're no different,

except in quality, from the snapshots of Dana I've taken
over twenty years
and put into our photo albums. I too marvel when

I open them and see
Dana young again—in that black bathing suit with the blue diagonal
stripe running over

full right breast, lean abdomen, to her left hip—fallen asleep
on a yellow and orange
lawn chair on the end of a dock. She's reclined the chair flat

to make a bed
surrounded on three sides by lake water. Two blue flip-flops stand
like empty footprints

next to a crumpled, wet, brown-and-white-striped towel. They are what's
left of those long summer days
I can't remember except for Dana lying there, white sunhat

slipped to one side
so I see each delicate ridge of her left ear's cartilage. One gold hoop
hangs from her earlobe

and catches the sunlight. She wears her long thick hair in two wet braids.
The swell of hip and breast
is a speedboat's wake rolling, undulating across the calm

lake to break against
a seawall. The water laps and laughs. Schools of minnows
dart and flash

through barred shadows under the dock. The whole bright day
comes back, contained
in the single angle of a snapshot. I dangle my feet over the edge

and the minnows swim up
to nibble them. Those small mouths make thirty simultaneous kisses.
They tickle until I can

hold still no longer. I flinch. They scatter. They are our twenty
summers, autumns,
winters, springs together. Here is Dana, eight months pregnant

with Lucy, our second daughter
who just turned twelve. Dana's standing in baggy blue tunic and matching
shorts on our front porch

in Salt Lake City, three houses ago. She wears owl-eye sunglasses
which reflect me taking
her picture and the two small squares of grass enclosed by concrete

that are our front yard.
Everything's doubled and distorted in those dark convex mirrors—
my head like a tadpole's,

bigger than my body. Why are there always two of me?
In the next moment
Dana will lift her blue tunic to show Eleanor, our older daughter,

her belly swollen into
a taut-skinned balloon, big as a globe of the world. Her navel is
the balloon's tied end.

In the photo Dana holds two red swollen tomatoes with green stems,
which she's just picked
from the garden, up to her breasts engorged beneath her blue tunic

and grins. One
of the tomatoes is so ripe its skin has split and spills
juice and seeds.

Dana's nipples are already leaking colostrum. In the next
snapshot, Eleanor
stands in the garden. She has wormed her way into an empty

tomato cage's cylinder
and twines her arms and legs around the rusted wire. She wants
to grow up fast,

leaf out, and be a green tomato ripening in the hot sun.
Every summer
Sargent and Nicola would visit Violet, Sargent's sister,

and her six children
"on the Continent." Nicola would remember, "One of my self-appointed
tasks was to carry them

about on my back. They are now quite grown up, of course, all but
one of them.
Rosemary, a sweetly beautiful girl, was killed by a bomb in one

of the air raids
on France." Beyond the bomb, Rose-Marie Ormond still stands
at seventeen in Sargent's

sketch, *The Cashmere Shawl*, watercolor and pencil on paper.
She's walking a garden path
in early spring. Only daffodils are flowering. The stucco wall

behind her is scribbled
with shadows. She wears a billowing white dress, has wrapped the shawl
tight around her waist

to show off her slimness, the fullness of her hips. It is a study
in cream, brown, beige, and taupe.
Head bound with a mauve scarf, she is swathed in her long dress

like a mummy. Hands
hidden. Only her face visible. Bronze hair, blue eyes gazing at something
beyond the picture.

What is that clotted turquoise blotch to the left of her head? A shadow,
the painter's too impetuous
brushstroke? Her dress blows in harsh March wind. Soon she will walk on.

XVII. Figure and Pool

John Singer Sargent
reclaimed his picture after the scandal and repainted Madame X's
fallen shoulder strap,

put it back in its "proper" position, over her shoulder blade, and never
exhibited anywhere
his album of nude male figure studies. I too hesitate to say

my love for men out loud,
that new desire I've only just discovered late in middle age
though it's always been

an underground river that ran beneath my adolescence. It percolated
through sandy soil
into hidden springs, wells, still pools I saw myself in

when I leaned close.
In my high school's cream-tiled shower room, I would imagine
naked women

to make my small prick start to swell, lengthen, and become as big
as those of my schoolmates, snapping
wet towels at each other. I watched them while they soaped chests, necks,

shoulders, arms, backs,
stomachs, buttocks. Rinsing off, they let the hot stream splurt
over their faces, across

torsos and thighs. Before toweling dry, they slapped the water
from their bodies.
Once the wrestling coach chose me as his partner to demonstrate

a quick escape.
He got down on hands and knees, had me grip him around the waist.
The room was humid

from sweating flesh. Steam hissed from rusted radiators. I felt
each inhalation of breath
expand his taut stomach beneath the damp gray T-shirt.

"Hold me harder," he roared.
"Don't hold me as if I were your girlfriend." The other wrestlers
snickered. I blushed

and clamped down. "That's better," he said. The boy I wanted to hold,
though I couldn't have said it then,
was my rival, Charlie Langtry, who was already taking calculus

and knew how to translate
Catullus. We were each assigned a poem to write out. "Just now
I surprised a darling boy

screwing my girlfriend, and I—may it please Venus—yoked myself
to them, ploughed him
with my hard cock." I went scarlet. I thought of how I'd fallen

for that schoolboy joke—"Bet you can't
bend over, look between your legs, and spell 'run' ten times as fast as you can."
"Are you in? Are you in?"

I'd stammered out before I got it and stopped. When the boys dared Charlie,
he merely laughed,
"Don't be so incurably vulgar!" He usually wore khaki pants, a wool

blazer that matched his rusty
auburn hair, which curled, I thought, like marble acanthus leaves
on Corinthian columns.

His wide blue eyes were more beautiful than any girl's. He had
bruised circles under them
from studying all night. He skipped his senior year to enter

Harvard, was first in our class
while I was always second. They called us "dorks" and "grinds." Too proud
and shy to talk to him,

I hated and adored him. In 1917, one year before
D'Inverno left Sargent,
they visited Villa Vizcaya, the Miami estate of millionaire

James Deering. Sargent painted
watercolors of Black workers swimming nude and lolling in the shallows.
The water laps

their hurdler's thighs. They lean back in the shade of mangrove trees.
One man straddles a smooth
driftwood log and stares in disbelief at the fully dressed

artist as if to say,
"Get rid of that ridiculous hat and shirt. Strip naked with us,
let the sun darken

your white skin." In another watercolor, a Black man stretches
full-length on his stomach
and gazes into a tidal pool that gives him back himself,

the pebbled bottom, the sun
behind purple clouds. Light and shadow dapple his bare back,
buttocks, and legs spread wide

into a wishbone's Y. Palms flat on hot sand, biceps flexed,
this Narcissus leans
down to kiss the self that trembles the tidal pool's still surface.

XVIII. Translation of Catullus's Poem 48

Your sweeter-than-pecan-pie
eyes, Juventius, if I could go on kissing continuously
them, I'd steal

three hundred thousand kisses and never think I was full, not even if
our kisses' harvest were
more numerous than the dried ears of feed corn in a silo.

XIX. David and Jonathan

"Thy love to me was wonderful, passing the love of women,"
so David mourned and tore
his clothes, wept and fasted after the death of Jonathan.

In his album of figure studies
Sargent drew four folios of draped figures he labeled
"Bible Illustrations."

Nicola as "David in the Camp of the Philistines"
is wrapped in a blanket,
stretches out on his side on a mountain top, props up his chin

and rests it on his left
palm. He gazes pensively across an invisible green valley
toward Judea, his homeland,

toward Jonathan. Does he remember how he would run his fingers
through Jonathan's long black hair
after making love? "And Jonathan stripped himself of the robe

that was upon him,
and gave it to David, and his garments, even to his sword,
and to his bow,

and to his girdle." David remembers kissing the rough black stubble
on Jonathan's cheek,
how Jonathan stood before him naked, unsheathed sword that made

him bleed when he tried
its sharpness against his thumb. He bent and strung the bow, plucked music
from it, one-stringed harp

that shot his arrow straight to its mark, a mountain goat leaping
rock to rock.
Wounded, it bounded off. David put on Jonathan's tunic

to which his scent still clung—
sweat, damp earth, crushed thyme. When Oscar Wilde was cross-examined,
he countered, "The 'Love that dare

not speak its name' in this century is such a great affection
of an elder for a younger
man as there was between David and Jonathan. . . ." Oscar wrote Bosie,

Lord Alfred Douglas, "Your love
has broad wings and is strong, your love comes to me through my prison
bars and comforts me,

your love is the light of all my hours." In the old photos of them
together, Bosie wears
boaters. Wilde leans toward him, slim boy, milk skin, blond hair, blue eyes.

His beauty still glows incandescent
from black-and-white studio portraits. Oscar called him "ivory and gilt."
Spoiled wild child, compulsive

gambler, rich man, youngest son of the ninth Marquess of Queensbury,
he sponged off Wilde,
introduced him to male prostitutes. For him Oscar deserted

his wife and two children,
then wrote to Robert Ross, his first lover and constant friend, "Bosie
is so tired: he lies

like a hyacinth on the sofa, and I worship him." The Marquess
of Queensbury threatened
his son, "I will give you the thrashing you deserve." Douglas

telegraphed his father,
"WHAT A FUNNY LITTLE MAN YOU ARE." He was only one inch
taller. High King Saul,

Jonathan's father, raged at his son's love for David. "Do not I know
that thou hast chosen the son
of Jesse to thine own confusion, and unto the confusion

of thy mother's nakedness?"
Saul wanted David dead. Queensbury left his calling card
at Wilde's Albemarle Club.

It said, "To Oscar Wilde posing Somdomite." He'd misspelled
that evil word.
As the Marquess hoped, Wilde sued for libel. He lost and was prosecuted

"for committing indecent acts"
with twelve men. He got two years, slept on a plank bed, picked oakum,
sewed postbags, walked

the treadmill for a month, ate beans and suet pudding, which brought on
"hose-down diarrhea."
Douglas, whom he had shielded at the trial, rented a yacht

and cabin boy.
Wilde commented, "Le prince du caprice est parti pour Capri."
When he got out of prison,

Bosie clamored to see him, but eventually deserted him,
as did most of his friends.
Wilde lived his remaining three years "in the Camp of the Philistines."

Only Robert Ross
and Reggie Turner, true Jonathans to his David, stayed with him
to the end. He was dying

of meningitis, an attack of the tertiary syphilis he'd contracted
at twenty-three
from a female prostitute. When morphine no longer killed the pain,

he drank champagne and told
his two friends, "I dreamt I was supping with the dead." Reggie replied,
"My dear Oscar,

you were probably the life and soul of the party!" When he died,
they said that "the body exploded
with fluids from the ear, nose, mouth, and other orifices."

Years later, Sargent
gave Robert Ross, who had presented his first European solo show
at Carfax Gallery,

a small bronze version of *Crucifixion*, his sculpture for the Boston
Public Library.
In low relief Christ stands on the coiled serpent. Under his arms

outstretched on a botonée cross
crouch naked Adam and Eve. They collect the blood that drips from his
nailed hands in two gold chalices.

Christ's lean arms embrace and shelter his cupbearers as if they were
two friends, two Ganymedes.
The three figures are bound together with one long winding sheet.

XX. Myths and Murals

Thomas Fox, architect
and technical consultant for Sargent's murals in Boston's Museum
of Fine Arts, remembered how

"on a hotel elevator he noticed that the operator, a young
colored man,
was possessed of a physique which he conceived would be of artistic

value. Most of those who saw…
the Museum murals in process learned that this young man served as the model
for practically all

the male figures, and indeed for some of the others." It was Fox's
decorous way of saying
that Thomas Eugene McKeller posed for female figures as well.

Women were "the others."
McKeller would model for Sargent for a year, but then was drafted
as a foot soldier

in the Great War. In 1916 he'd gotten the job at the Hotel Vendome,
where Sargent often stayed,
and wore an elevator man's black cap and matching

double-breasted suit with brass
buttons and three gold stripes around both sleeves' wool cuffs. He ironed
his pants so the crease

was a bayonet's edge and shined his shoes until he could see himself
in their black wingtips.
"What floor, sir?" he had asked. "Oh, the floor be damned!" Sargent replied.

"Look here, my man, would you like
to earn some money on the side and do a little moonlighting?"
Fox and Nicola,

who was carrying his master's valises, looked the other way.
For five years Sargent painted
his white Apollo, Hercules, Orestes, and Atlas, using McKeller

as his Black model.
One art critic says that Sargent "transformed and idealized"
Thomas, meaning that

the artist bleached and whitewashed his skin, thinned his full lips,
gave him blond hair,
blue eyes, Aryanized him. But his face and lean, forced-march-hardened

body remain.
Walk around the rotunda and down the cream marble staircase, see
beneath the mythic themes

in blue and gold how Thomas E. McKeller's face looks back
from both men and women,
from Athena and Achilles, from Perseus, from Medusa's

severed, snake-haired head.
It is a hall of mirrors and terrors. In *Orestes Pursued*
by the Furies, naked

peroxide-blond McKeller runs from twelve robed female figures,
each of whose staring, speechless
faces is his own. They hold out asps to bite him, lift torches

toward his shadowed
face, which he shields with his left hand. He stretches out his bloody
right hand as if to say

help or stop. The mother he has murdered grasps her gashed breast
to staunch the blood.
She stares him down. Her shocked, accusing face is his. What would

my eighty-nine-year-old
mother say if I told her I love men? Would it kill her?
Or would she say, "I've known

for a long time. You shouldn't worry so..."? Twenty feet away,
Thomas McKeller as Hercules
battles the Hydra that's wrapped blue-green and rust-brown coils around

his muscled body. It is
the second labor. He wears the impenetrable Nemean lion's
skin. The great beast's forepaws

are knotted over his chest. Its head is a hood from which McKeller
stares impassively
out of the lion's open snarling mouth at the fire-fanged

snake he holds
in his left hand. The Hydra's thirteen deadly snake heads twine
like vines around him,

hiss, breathe fire, and seem to grow from his own loins and buttocks.
They are a many-headed
phallus that rises, rages, will not be subdued by the knotty

cudgel raised
in McKeller's right hand. From each head he whacks off, two more writhing
snakes will come.

He's wrestling with himself. The blue-green Hydra is sexuality's
earth power that no sky god
or his son can conquer. Walk on, see how the Danaïdes carry

earthen vessels of water
on their heads and pour them into a leaky urn. They are in hell
because they've stabbed with daggers

their forty-nine husbands on their one mass-wedding night. The water
streams from the urn's
three gargoyle mouths, which say that violence within a marriage

can never be forgiven.
After committing murder, the self is a cracked urn. Desire's cold
underworld well water

passes through the fired clay. After betrayal, the betrayer
goes thirsty, must carry
the water she'll never drink and let it spill on the ground.

Sargent painted the Danaïdes
in white sleeveless tunics on a blue-gray background. He is said
to have used chorus girls

from the Ziegfeld Follies as models, but those water-carriers
have McKeller's broad shoulders
and sinewed arms. So does Atlas who, halfway down the hall, holds

the heavens on his bowed
back. The sun rises behind him. At his feet, the seven naked nymphs
of the Hesperides

embrace and fall asleep, arms and legs entwined around each other.
Two of them,
for whom McKeller posed at the Columbus Avenue studio,

hold the golden apples
of immortality, which they have picked—bocci balls that match
their fire-bright hair.

Atlas lifts the constellations, a golden zodiac upon
his straining back.
Here's the soft-shell crab, sign I was born under, and there's

Taurus, the bull whose patient
strength I need. Between them, the Heavenly Twins—Castor the horse tamer
and Pollux the boxer—

lean naked against each other above McKeller's shoulder. They are
inseparable.
Did Sargent fall in love with Thomas E. McKeller? Everywhere

Sargent looked, he saw
Thomas. And what of Nicola? He carried his master's monogrammed
suitcases out of the elevator

and into the four-room suite on the fifth floor. Sargent kept drawing
          and painting Thomas.
He is Prometheus chained to a rock. The vulture hovers over him

          and eats his liver.
Its outspread left wing covers his naked buttocks. He posed
          as Ganymede who throws

his arms around the eagle's white-feathered neck in terror
          when it lifts him
skyward. Its talons dig into his hips. High art is rape.

XXI. "This was my body..."

          To supplement his income
of fifty dollars per month as an elevator operator and the five
          dollars per day

that Sargent paid him for modeling, Thomas E. McKeller
          performed part-time
as a contortionist. Working the crowd on Washington St.

          in Boston's Black
South End, McKeller in red leotard would lie face-down on park grass,
          bend his legs back

over his head until the backs of his thighs rested on his shoulders.
          He wrapped
legs like arms around his neck. He coiled about himself,

          writhed into
a standing position, torso so lithe his head appeared right-side-up
          between his legs

and emerged from his crotch as if he were birthing himself.
          People shrieked
or watched mesmerized. He tied himself in knots

until it was impossible
to tell one body part from another. The crowd rained silver
coins into his black

derby. At eight years old in Wilmington, North Carolina,
he'd seen
white vigilantes burn Black businesses, kill three hundred

Black men and women
with a Gatling gun. He'd squeezed himself under white
picket fences

to escape white boys with baseball bats. One hundred and four
years later,
his great-niece Deidre would recall the family legend,

"I think
Thomas McKeller left the South because there was a question
as to whether

he was gay or not. And for his safety it was much better for him
to leave the South
than to stay there." What did he think when Sargent sketched his torso,

then put the Apollo Belvedere's
head, with sun's halo like a thin cross-section of lemon, upon his shoulders,
erased his Black skin,

and set him in the center of a circle of nine mincing, Caucasian
muses he'd also
modeled for, naked, wearing cheesecloth falsies? Was it all

part of his contortionist's
act? Was he the chameleon that adopts protective coloration to survive,
stays invisible? Sargent

couldn't paint or draw without him, wrote to his friend Fox, "I wonder
what has become
of that darkey model—if he should turn up again,

or if you have
his address you might let him know that I want him—" Thomas may
have frowned, then laughed

as he gazed up at the Museum of Fine Arts' rotunda to see
the swell of his Black biceps
in all those gods' and goddesses' smooth white arms. Proud and angry,

he'd recall, "During my services
I believe I became his main model…Atlas with the world on his shoulders
this was my body except my head."

XXII. Nude Study of Thomas E. McKeller

Among those many academic
studies, Sargent let himself forget the old myths once and painted
Thomas E. McKeller

as he truly saw him. The Black man has stripped off and thrown
to the studio floor
his elevator operator's pressed suit. He sits on a large green cushion

slightly askew
upon the modeling stand. The knee of his right leg bent back
under him rests

on a small brownish pillow. His thighs are flexed. He pushes
himself upward
from palms flat on the cushion behind his buttocks. He looks left,

lifts his chin
so his long lean black swan's neck is visible in reddish-brown
glory, shadows that define

jawbone and Adam's apple, green stippling catching perfectly
the five o'clock stubble
on his raised right cheek. His left leg dangles over the edge of the modeling

stand, bends backwards.
His skin glows one hundred shades of brown. It's almost buttery
where sun through skylight

strikes his sternum. His smooth hairless thighs are the color
of raw almonds stripped
from their shells. The pit of his stomach is mahogany sanded down

and polished. His ribcage
is oiled rosewood. His slant left nipple is the dark brown of Brazilian
coffee beans, his right

the color of unhulled cashews. His body is a psalm sung
by John Singer Sargent's
softest camel-hair brush. Bristly pubic hair glistens black

like Persian lambswool.
Thick, uncircumcised cock and scrotum are gray-black as volcanic
ash. Behind his wide

shoulders outlined with a thread of vermilion lies a blue-gray
circle that encloses
Thomas's whole body. It's the roundel Sargent was painting

for Prometheus, thief
of fire, before Thomas's beauty made him hold his breath and paint
the Black man's body

unwhitened. The avenging vulture's quick-brushed, reddish
wings, half-painted over
with cobalt mixed with titanium white, surround

Thomas's torso.
They have become his wings, sprout from his shoulder blades. They lift
him up. "Your love

has broad wings," Wilde still whispers to Bosie, "and is strong, your love
comes to me through
my prison bars." Those wings were Sargent's lust for Thomas.

They could not free
either man. Sargent would never exhibit the canvas. Thomas put back on
the elevator man's

black uniform. In the painting, to the left of Thomas, sits a blurred
figure looking down.
It is an earlier pose that Sargent painted over. It still

shows through. It is
history's shadow. It chains us to the rock. It lets the vulture
eat his fill, devour

our inner organs. No one walks away unhurt. But here
Thomas gazes upward.
In the twentieth century's shadow, Sargent painted a naked Black man

whose right ear catches
sunlight and glows like barrier-reef coral, pure rhododendron red.
That brush kissed this ear.

XXIII. Suppose

Suppose desire is here only by being not here. It leaves its invisible
unmistakable
trace. Suppose you camouflage desire. Smuggle the beautiful

body of a Black man
into your white fiction, where only those in the know will notice him.
Suppose

you erase the beloved's skin color and put him in murals chockablock
with old Greek myths
to hide your own desire. But then you lose forever

who the beloved is.
He cannot speak. Cannot say or gainsay his side
of absence's story.

XXIV. "Thou Shalt Not Steal"

Nicola left Sargent
in early 1918. He couldn't stand to sit by and watch
Sargent at sixty-two

go gaga with unrequited love for Thomas, moon over him
by day, daydream
of him all night. It wasn't right. Nicola's official story

was that in America
he'd got the "money fever." He wanted to be a studio photographer,
asked Sargent for a raise.

"He would not pay the price and we parted, with a little pain
on both sides,
but with no ill feeling on either." Nicola was not a complete

liar. They'd had
an argument. Sargent had asked McKeller to go to dinner
at the Copley Plaza.

"You can't do that," said Nicola. "That nigger's just your model."
Sargent spluttered,
"Damn! Damn! Damn!" Nicola walked out, went to the track,

bet his month's pay "on the ponies,"
lost. He got drunk in a hotel bar, tried to pick up the bartender, the wrong
right man. "You fucking pouf!"

the man he'd hit on shouted. "Say that again!" Nicola replied
and swung. He got another
"beautiful black eye," but knocked the bartender out cold. The man didn't

come out of his coma
for three weeks. Charges were filed. Worried about his reputation,
Sargent dismissed

Nicola, who pleaded to come back. Sargent refused
to see him. Years later,
Nicola would say, "The only priceless thing in my possession

is the recommendation
John Singer Sargent wrote for me on the note paper
of the Copley Plaza Hotel."

It took him all day to write it. The letter began, "It grieves me
no end to lose
Nicola D'Inverno, my model, valet, and house manager

for twenty-five years."
It ended, "He is every inch a man." Commissioned by the government
"as an official war artist

to memorialize the joint efforts of English and American
troops," Sargent left
for France and the front. He painted *Gassed*, a twenty-foot canvas showing

a line of nine blindfold-bandaged
soldiers being led, hands on each other's shoulders, by medics
to a dressing station after

an attack of mustard gas. It is sunset. The men walk across
a flat, bombed-out
plain, where other wounded, blindfolded soldiers lie huddled together.

They turn toward the sun
they cannot see. The canvas is a monotonous monochrome
of browns and golden ochers.

Sky whitens to faded khaki, the same shade as the doughboys'
uniforms. The ground
is stained sepia. One medic tells them, "Watch your step!"

as they go
from the dirt onto a low plank walkway. One soldier lifts his boot
a foot and a half off the ground

so his right leg makes a right angle. He doesn't know how high
the walkway is,
doesn't want to stumble. As in Bruegel, as in Luke's gospel, the blind lead

the blind. When *Gassed*
was first exhibited, some of the viewers fainted. Sargent stayed
in a fieldstone house

whose windows had been blasted out. He was so naïve that when
he heard the military band
playing one Sunday, he remarked, "I suppose there is no fighting

on the Sabbath."
Between trips to the front, he painted watercolors of young soldiers
swimming naked

in a river near Arras. They lie on the bank, smoke cigarettes,
sunbathe, talk.
Against the long, rough, dark green grasses their bodies shine white.

Sunlight like a hand
caressing their chests and thighs is tremulous as if it knows
these boys are "cannon fodder."

In one watercolor two boys have fallen asleep together.
One rests on his stomach,
the other sprawls on his back. Their two heads seem to touch. The grass's

shadows stripe their legs
with lash marks. Sargent also painted two fully dressed doughboys
surreptitiously picking

ripe black plums. One boy puts the fruit into his watering
mouth with his right hand,
is about to bite down, feel the juice spurt over his tongue and fill

his mouth with taste's
indescribable decibels, a loud red sound. He looks quickly
to the right to see

if anyone is watching them. The other boy wears a Highlander's kilt
    and has his back to us.
He reaches up with both hands to pull the black plums down, making

    his kilt rise and shorten
into a pleated miniskirt. His buttocks are full, almost womanly.
    Sunlight leaves its handprint

on that kilt. Sargent has titled the watercolor "*Thou Shalt Not*
    Steal." Commandments must
be broken. These two Adams eating their fill from the Tree of Knowledge

    are D'Inverno and Sargent.
The forbidden plums they bite into are the twenty-five years they've lived
    together despite

the Criminal Law Amendment Act of 1885,
    which prohibited
"the commission by any male person of any act of gross

    indecency with another
male person." Queen Victoria, informed by her advisors
    that the law did not apply

to women, retorted, "No woman would do that!" The watercolor
    rejoices in stolen
pleasures, in the bare backs of a man's legs under his raised

    kilt. Sargent's gaze
is that of a tender voyeur, the outsider looking in at what
    he once had and will never

possess again. Does the picture encompass his longing for Thomas,
    who was thirty-four years
younger? Does "*Thou Shalt Not Steal*" declare his guilty love for the beautiful

    young man he couldn't
have? The plum tree's dense green leaves are chinked with light. Always
    the mesmeric swing of that kilt.

XXV. Conversation, Not in a Painting

—You've been down in the basement, writing a poem about dicks, for the last three months. When are you going to come up?

—I don't know.

—When you do come up, will you come up as a gay man?

—I don't know.

—I think you want to stay in the basement and not let anyone know what you're writing.

—No.

—How do you think it makes me feel, knowing that you're down in that basement and beat off to naked men?

—That's not what I'm doing in the basement.

—What are you doing?

—I'm trying to write a poem about who I am. To write it, I have to go down into the basement every day.

—This isn't a marriage. I want someone I can make plans with, grow old with. I don't want to live in your basement.

—The basement is often dark. It's hard to see down there. The furnace, with its steady blue pilot light, keeps the room warm.

—Oh, let's stop talking in metaphors.

—That's hard not to do.

—I think you're waiting for me to find someone else so that you can leave this marriage gracefully.

—No. I am trying to write a poem.

—I think you're foolish.

—I am foolish. I like being able to see all the drainage and water pipes, the heating ducts, that run through the basement's ceiling.

—Stop it.

—Sorry.

—Are you attracted to someone else?

—I look at both men and women, if that's what you mean, and find them desirable.

—No, it's not what I mean. Do you have someone in mind?

—No.

—You're staying in the marriage for the sake of our daughters?

—Partly. I love them.

—When they grow up and are gone, you'll leave me.

—No.

—Do you have any idea what it would be like to be a woman who's single and sixty? I'll have to get a tummy tuck.

—I love you.

—It would be better if you left me now rather than later.

—Is that what you want?

—No.

—What do you want?

—I want a husband. What do you want?

—I would like to know what it's like to make love to men. But I also know my desire hurts you. It's best not to talk about it.

—But we are talking about it.

—I know.

—What do you want?

—I'd like to stay in our marriage. Because we are so close to each other, I will always be torn.

—No, what do you want to do?

—I don't know. Wait.

—I can't wait. I need to know, to be sure.

—I don't know if I'll ever be sure. Often, foolishly, I think I don't know anything about myself.

—That's rubbish.

—Well, it's my rubbish then.

—If you left me, I would be devastated.

—If I left you, I would be devastated.

—That's two of us.

—If I said there are many fuses in the fuse box in the basement, but that you're the circuit breaker…

—That would be pure cornball. Just as if I were to say that all electrical systems need to be grounded. Here we are, talking metaphors again.

—What else is there?

—Sex.

—Yes?

—Yes.

XXVI. Crescenzo Fusciardi

For the last two years I've looked at John Singer Sargent's oils,
                    watercolors, charcoals
and found myself, all my desires and contradictions, contained

                    within his canvases and works
on paper, his album of figure studies. Looking is my way
                    of discovering, uncovering,

inventing a new self. In the Fogg Art Museum's viewing room
                    I take each charcoal drawing,
lift the cream matting that keeps it flat, peel back the tracing paper

                    to reveal the nude male figures,
the shapes desire can take. Here a model sprawls on his back,
                    the bed unmade, hands clasped

above his head, ribcage thrust upwards, stomach concave, buttocks
                    raised high on pillows
they sink into, scrotum's smooth leather pouch loose around

                    testicles, prick
like a thick forefinger, legs hanging off the bed, the body spent,
                    head turned away

in a languor there is no one word for. I can't see his face.
Ecstasy is always
nameless. We are "put out of place" and lose ourselves

for a few minutes that last
hours. We are remade, made new. To die "the little death,"
"come" into being,

to be emptied and filled, to become a white vase holding long green stems
of fire-tongued freesias
on the bedside table. To become a car alarm that wakes everyone

with its wild honking,
Mozart's lost cadenza for car horn, the silence after it stops,
and then the stolen vehicle

that five teenagers joyride with the top down across a swaying suspension
bridge, whose cables choir,
wail in the wind, catch and hold the full moon's litter, its paper

picnic plate. Ecstasy is
breaking and entering, our house burgled, all the drawers dumped
on the floor—wrenches,

camisoles, tape measures, CDs, bobby pins, step-great-grandmother's
vine-twined silverware,
potting soil, all thrown together like party mix and nothing

missing. This joy
gang-tackles us when we make love. It's Dana's and mine. It's Sargent's
and Nicola's. It's

that of the two women—one with a crew cut, the other with spiked
purple hair—soul-kissing
each other goodbye after their breakfast of Dobos torte, blueberry

scone, and black coffee
at Rosalie's Bakery. They have to go to work. They stand on the corner,
beside the graffiti-scrawled

stop sign, tongues like naked pearl divers holding their breaths as they
            dive down together to the deepest
oyster bed. One takes the other's face between her hands.

            They kiss for thirty seconds
before they surface. They walk away without looking back. But if
            ecstasy's a far country

beyond names, we go there with lovers whose names we repeat like mantras
            leading us
to bliss and back. Dana. Nicola. Thomas Eugene McKeller.

            Every day should be
St. Valentine's. Sargent drew twenty-year-old Crescenzo Fusciardi's
            head and naked shoulders

with quick incisive charcoal lines for breastbone, nostrils, nose,
            left ear's rim, right side
of face, eyebrows, but smudged his soft girl skin around the strong

            left jawbone, chin, the neck's
tendons, his eyelids—those places made for kissing. His hair is long,
            rough cut, bed-kempt. Black eyes

hold their steady stare off to the right, are large and liquid
            as a doe's. Light glints
from upper lip. Under his few scraggly chest hairs, Sargent has written

            his name and address,
32 Great Bath St., Clerkenwell. He was a friend
            of Nicola's. His face—

die-cast steel, an opening white narcissus—is that of the young man
            in tight black leather pants
I pass on the street as I leave the museum. I glance at his crotch

            and blush. His stare scorches
through me. "Hello," it says, "I'm hanging loose and full of juice."
            I cannot look away.

XXVII. Ruckus

"Crescenzo" and "crescendo" both mean "growing," either the music's
volume or a man's
height, girth, brawn. What new self am I growing into? Who am I

crescendoing toward?
I love women, long for men. Am I a coward when it comes to love?
Next summer I'll turn fifty.

Even if I were free, what young Crescenzo Fusciardi would
have me? And if I could
make love to men, wouldn't I want to return to Dana? These are all

the wrong questions.
No canvas, watercolor, charcoal study will help me live
my bisexual life.

What I need is music. What does Madame X's bright red ear
above her neck's livid
lavender-tinged skin hear? It's the flamenco singer and guitarists,

the dancer's black high heels'
tattoo, their stuttering staccato thunder upon the floorboards
of the dance hall in Sargent's

wall-length oil on canvas, *El Jaleo*. The title of a fast Andalusian dance,
"el jaleo" also means
"ruckus." It refers to the hand clapping, finger snapping,

boot stomping, olé shouting
that always accompany the true flamenco. *Así se toca!*
Vamanos, Manitas de Plata!

"That's the way to touch those strings! Silver Hands, let's go!"
What I need
is ruckus—*Si, Senior, eso es!* "Yes, sir, that's it!"—

and the saeta singer's
wordless wail. An art that rises from the gut, a voice that screams,
groans, grieves, and makes

music from the ruckus of my life. To be that dancer,
leaning backwards
as she hurls herself forward, throwing huge shadows on the wall

while she whirls her white dress out,
whips and flings her black shawl's frenzied fringes left and right
to the raw rhythms

the two guitarists strum. *When I see him in the street   He makes*
me tremble. Five men
in black sombreros and two women in red shawls sit in a row

on rush-bottomed chairs
against the gray wall. Their lifted, clapping hands cast shadows
of wolves and flying crows

across the wall. *I dug a hole in the sand   And there I buried*
my thoughts.   Then I threw
myself in   So no one else should suffer. To the left of one guitarist's

head, someone has stamped
his red palm print upon the wall. *Because nobody loves you*
You feel like you're made of stone.

The singer improvises pain, whispers, then yells, *Ayi!*
Ayi! But humor
must enter the song too. *I'm moving out tonight,   I'm taking all*

my things   Including
the cooking pot...We each make our own ruckus, the two pretty
young women, whose red shawls

are the only spot of color this late at night, yell, *Give me a heel*
So I can stamp my feet!
In the row of listeners, some clapping, some shouting, *Bueno! Olé!*

or *Ponle corazón!*,
some sitting silent, there is one empty chair. Upon it a blood orange,
or is it a votive candle

burning in an amber glass cylinder? Absence is flame
and fruit. *The wound*
in my heart is now bleeding through my mouth. One man holds his guitar

flat on his lap.
His eyes are closed. He doesn't play. *Oh, how my bones ache,*
But they stop aching when

I sing... All true singers are possessed by fire and, even
as they are consumed,
sing the fire's sweetness, the section of blood orange between

their teeth before
they bite down. It has not been granted to everyone to know
the love of men

and women. Bless the gift and the giver, sings the singer. *The guitar*
is from Morón,   The rhythm
from Jerez;   The feeling is from Seville   And from Triana

all the rest.
The singer sits at the exact center of the picture. The neck and tuning
pegs of his neighbor's

guitar stretch across his white-shirted chest and are silhouetted
like a black hand
or claw print. Light flashes from the two guitars' soundboxes,

from the flying folds
of the dancer's dress, from the fandango her white fan beats out between
her thumb and first two fingers.

A cigarillo has fallen to the floor. It's still smoldering.
A bit of black fringe
ripped from the dancer's shawl in her frenzy has also come to rest

on the dusty floorboards.
The singer throws his head back against the wall. His shadow
haloes his head.

We see only the muscles swell in his throat, the dark O of mouth
through which sound pours.
It is as if the moment of full song and orgasm are the same.

XXVIII. Uno Sombrero para Viaje

Sargent drew the first
two sketches for *El Jaleo* on the back of a receipt for
a sombrero. He didn't

have any other paper with him in the Café El Gallo at midnight
in Madrid. It took him
three minutes to scrawl in black ink the high-heeled dancer, her two

guitarristas, the row
of men and women clapping in their chairs pushed back against
the wall. But then the music

changed to a farruca. A man in tight black pants, short vest,
white shirt, and a sombrero
of black velvet spangled with silver shooting stars like spurs

digging into a stallion's
sweaty hide stood up and took the floor. His heels pounded out
machine-gun fire

in a zapateado, footwork that was fireworks. Sargent ripped
the receipt in two
and drew on the lower half with dark brown ink and a wash of sepia

the strutting dancer,
his buttocks arched backwards, arms raised over his head, fingers
snapping castanets.

All he lacked to be cock of El Gallo that Saturday night
was a red rose
clenched between his teeth. Why did Sargent make the dancer

in his ruckus on canvas
a woman? Was it propriety or did the dancer's white dress
provide more drama

against the row of black-clad men? White silk's voluminous folds,
its spiral swirls
as the dancer lifts her hem, hold mysteries more manifold

than any man's pants.
I want to put the two torn halves of the receipt together
so the man and woman

dance together, the woman above the man. Flip the sketches over,
read the full
receipt from Senior Villasante's shop at 38 Alacalá St.

The date has been left blank.
"From Mr. Sargent, for one traveling sombrero at 60 reales,
I have received

payment." It's signed by Juan Solar. *Uno sombrero para viaje.* One
sombrero for journeying,
what did it look like? I imagine a purple velvet hat

with embroidered gold petals
on the wide brim around the crown so it becomes an opening
crocus. It might

have been a straw sombrero with concentric rings
of bull's-eye colors—
red, yellow, blue, and green around the floppy brim

two and a half feet
in diameter. Put it on, transform yourself into the sun
or a giant walking lollipop!

It was black velvet with a thin band of silver around the crown.
It shaded his face
as he journeyed on through Jerez, Seville, and Triana to Morón.

XXIX. Drag Queen

"Let's give it up
for the one and only Chantrelle!" yells the drag show's emcee
and the ballroom goes wild,

everyone on their feet, screaming, swaying to Aretha's
"R.E.S.P.E.C.T."
while a single spotlight picks out the Black queen in a leopard-skin

miniskirt, stiletto heels,
pink fishnet stockings, and black-on-white, polka-dotted bikini top
filled with the opulent

swell of her fake breasts. She's shaved her long lean legs and wears
a platinum blonde wig.
She minces down the runway. Her hips lip-sync to the bass's backbeat.

High camp, the illusion
is almost perfect. The crowd chants, "Chantrelle! Chantrelle!" A woman
shouts to her neighbor,

"I hate it when drag queens have better bodies than we do!" I remember
how at five years old
I snuck into my mother's bedroom, shut the door, stripped naked,

dressed up in her panties and bra,
and danced before the full-length mirror, wiggling my scrawny butt.
I wanted to be her.

I loved the cool smooth feel of silk against my crotch,
empty scrotum,
undescended testicles. What would it be like not to have

a penis? I pulled
my small prick back between my legs and closed them. Presto,
it vanished. I could imagine

I had a vagina. The mirror did not lie. I was a girl.
Deliciousness
of otherness. To step out of one body and become another,

to strut, teeter
in high heels down the strobe-lit runway, disco ball scattering
shattered light around

the huge ballroom, to know that two hundred men are looking
only at me
as I shimmy, shake, and sway, fling my flaming, flamingo-pink

feather boa over
one bare shoulder with a sultry stare, high-kick like an awkward
chorus girl, almost

trip, make them laugh at my faux pas, then stop to readjust my wig.
I'd bump and grind
to "I can't get no satisfaction," give them two hundred

hard-ons. My mother
opened the shut door, caught me wearing her too-big purple panties,
her plunge-line 36-C bra

filled only with air. "What are you doing?" she shouted. "Put on your proper
clothes. Don't ever let
me catch you dressed in my underwear again!" I blushed, stammered,

and obeyed.
But here's Chantrelle, lip-syncing for us, "There's a rose in black at Spanish
Harlem." She wears a pink

garter belt and matching thong, which the crowd has stuffed with dollar bills.
It does not hide her hard-on.
"The glory of God," Saint Irenaeus wrote, "is the man fully alive."

XXX. Male Venus Rising with One Black Leather Glove

The self is ineluctable,
multiple, silver precipitate from a dark solution. I contain
not multitudes

but several selves, not one deeper or more true than another.
Myself, what is that?
It is all these perfumes, distillations, essences together.

Breathe in, smell them,
celebrate all of them, down to the least whiff of brine
and wrack oozing up

from a saltwater swamp. Sing equally the lavender
eau de toilette
distilled from the bright blue fields of Provence bordered with sunflowers

and the stink of oil refineries
along New Jersey's Garden State Parkway, that "world fart"
as Dana calls it.

Old world, new world, which is it? Thoreau said "to cut a broad
swath and shave close,
to drive life into a corner, and reduce it to its lowest terms,

and, if it proved to be mean,
why then to get the whole and genuine meanness of it..." And even
a child molester must be

not wholly mean. Somewhere, sheltering inside him, crouches the child
crying, bleeding
from his rectum. And even the saint is not wholly holy, but is

perhaps a glutton
like Sargent. He could not stop eating, stuffed himself with mutton,
Parker House rolls,

whipped mashed potatoes, wild rice, yams, calves' brains in black butter,
sweetbreads, oysters.
One sitter said, "My idol ate during the best part of two hours

(dinners were lengthy in those days)
with a steadfastness and a concentration such as I have never
before or since seen equaled

at a meal." The self shall not make unto itself any graven
images. And yet
one of my selves will always be Nicola D'Inverno posing

for Sargent after a heavy
lunch of pasta puttanesca, salad, French bread, Beaujolais,
brie, and raspberry fool.

He is naked except for one black leather glove on his right hand.
The glove makes him
all the more naked. The muscles in his thighs have gone to fat.

He has a double chin,
but his biceps still bulge. He must be nearly forty. He sits on a settee
covered with a dustcloth,

leans back against a huge, hot pink, satin pillow. It frames his upper
body. His left arm curls
over the top and back of his head like a parenthesis.

He rests his right arm
against the pillow so it makes an L. His body is still
beautiful cursive.

He has a bristly Chaplinesque mustache. His bedroom eyes
under their thick eyebrows
are dreamy and almost shut. He's splayed the fingers of his one

black leather glove apart
so his upturned palm becomes a three-lobed sassafras leaf.
His legs are angled left

so we see only dark brown pubic hair. He could be
a Venus by Rubens
floating on a pink cloud the color of raspberry fool.

Look closely.
You can see part of the long shank of his prick playing peekaboo
over the top of his left thigh.

The painting is meant to be a tease. On the wall behind Nicola
hangs a gilt-framed oil.
It's some indecipherable sky and landscape. It says only

that our lives are all
illusion, paintings within paintings. Sargent puffs on his cigar,
blows smoke rings.

To pass the time, they make up more bad jokes. "—Knock, knock!
—Who's there?
—Madame X! —Madame X who? —Madame, excuse

my farting please!"
They snort with laughter. Sargent rests his hand on Nicola's thigh
plush against the dustcloth.

XXXI. Nicola D'Inverno Photographs Sargent Painting in the Alps, 1911

It must be high
summer and over seven thousand feet, somewhere above
the Simplon Pass.

Nicola has set up two giant white umbrellas before and behind
Sargent to diffuse
the noon light he paints by, make it less harsh. They protect him

from wind. The artist
sits on a broad rock, right hand raised, about to dip the brush
into his rectangular

watercolor pan, dab rag paper with pink wildflowers sprung
from crevices
in huge gray boulders. Though Nicola's photo is black-and-white,

I imagine Sargent
wears a yellow wool jacket with matching vest buttoned tight
across his protruding

belly. He sports a high-crowned, white sun hat whose brim
casts a diagonal
shadow so we do not see his eyes, only the profile of his

grizzle-bearded face
from nose to chin. Nicola has framed him against one of the white
umbrellas. Sargent

sits upright at its center in the same way
yellow stamens
rise from white petals of alpine anemones. One observer said

that Sargent between
the two umbrellas gave the appearance of being "a newly
hatched chicken,

surrounded by broken eggshells." One does not have
to look long
or hard to see that this grainy photo shows

Nicola's love
as clearly as Sargent's watercolor brush would cherish
one year later

the sunlight falling on Nicola's shoulders and thighs
as he sits naked,
dangles his legs into a mountain stream. He still braces himself

with both hands,
on violet-shadowed rocks, leans back against cold water's
rush and thrash.

Coda: *Reverie*

2021

No one can tell
anyone else what to do with the life we've unaccountably
been given. I

have chosen this apartment, its one large room lit by a wide
window that looks out
on a long river that passes ceaselessly under two bridges.

One bridge for
pedestrians. The other for cars, two lanes each way. It is winter.
Nine inches of subzero

wind-sculpted snow. The river almost frozen over. One black
stream, the central
channel between ice sheets that extend whitely inwards

from steep banks
towards that dark center. It is late. The streetlights have come on. But I
do not turn on

my reading lamp. I like to watch how the darkness comes.
As if an artist's
invisible hand were gradually filling in a white page

with a charcoal stick's shadings
until the page vanishes. And there is only night. And the shapes within
that austere

darkness clarify. A scraggly row of trees along the silently
muttering river.
Cars' headlights crossing one of two bridges. Then taillights. One

pedestrian walking
across the other bridge home. If I were that pedestrian, if I had
the eloquence

of the river, I would tell you how I got here. But I lack
the river's grand
periodic sentence that never stops. I could say I have been

divorced
now for one long year. I could say that after my brother's death
I saw

how short my life is. I wanted its innumerable moments to accumulate
like snow. There is a red
poinsettia by my window in a green plastic pot wrapped in gold

foil. One spot of frail
blood against vast winter whiteness under streetlights. Below my window
countless footprints

crisscross each other's paths. Meet and depart. Where are they
going? I couldn't
tell you whether they are coming or going in all these tons of still

snow, a silence
that has fallen on us unexpectedly out of clear sky. I am entering
old age.

My hair has turned white overnight with the years' slow snowfall.
At twenty
John Singer Sargent painted *Young Man in Reverie*. It shows

a black-haired
man with his first wispy mustache, who leans against a wall
white as tonight's

new snow. He is naked underneath a brown cloak that has fallen
and exposed his left
shoulder. On a white projection from the white wall

stand three white
vases. One has a few light blue markings, which the artist
has indicated

with an inspired scherzo of quick brushstrokes. We are fragile as
 those vases.
Who will fill our fired clay with clear cold water? From what well?

 And drink from us
until they know thirst no longer? See how the vessels
 they have drunk from

remain full, brim over with lip-lapping well water. Sargent painted
 that young man
in reverie on the island of Capri. I too was once that beautiful.

A PORTFOLIO OF IMAGES

Works by John Singer Sargent

Reclining Male Nude (Nicola D'Inverno) c. 1890–1915
Charcoal on off-white laid paper, 18$\frac{3}{4}$ × 24$\frac{9}{16}$ inches
Harvard Art Museums/Fogg Museum, Gift of Mrs. Francis Ormond

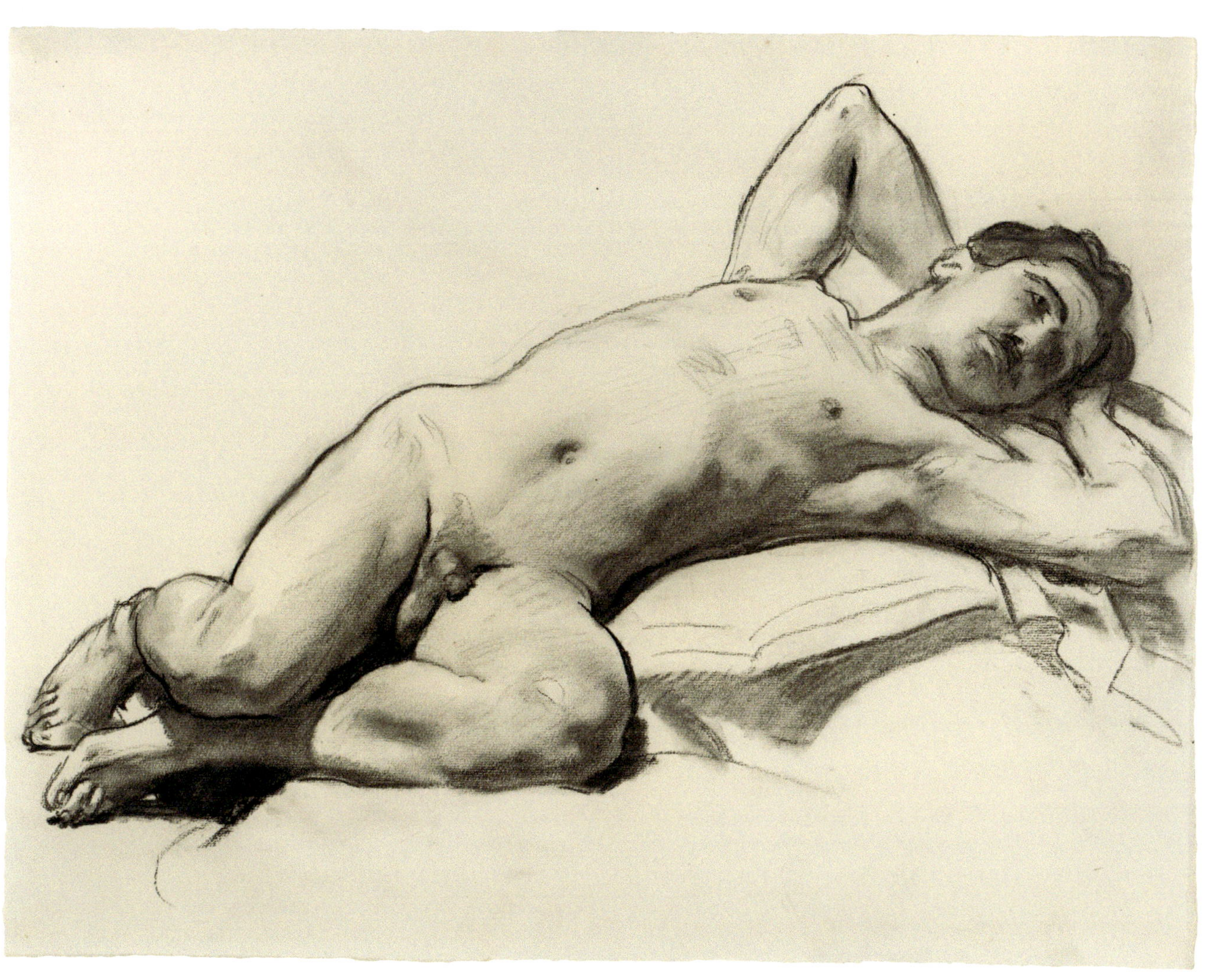

Male Nude Seen from Behind, Arm Raised Over Head c. 1890–1915

Charcoal on off-white laid paper, 24 5/16 × 19 inches

Harvard Art Museums/Fogg Museum, Gift of Mrs. Francis Ormond

Photograph © President and Fellows of Harvard College, 1937.9.24

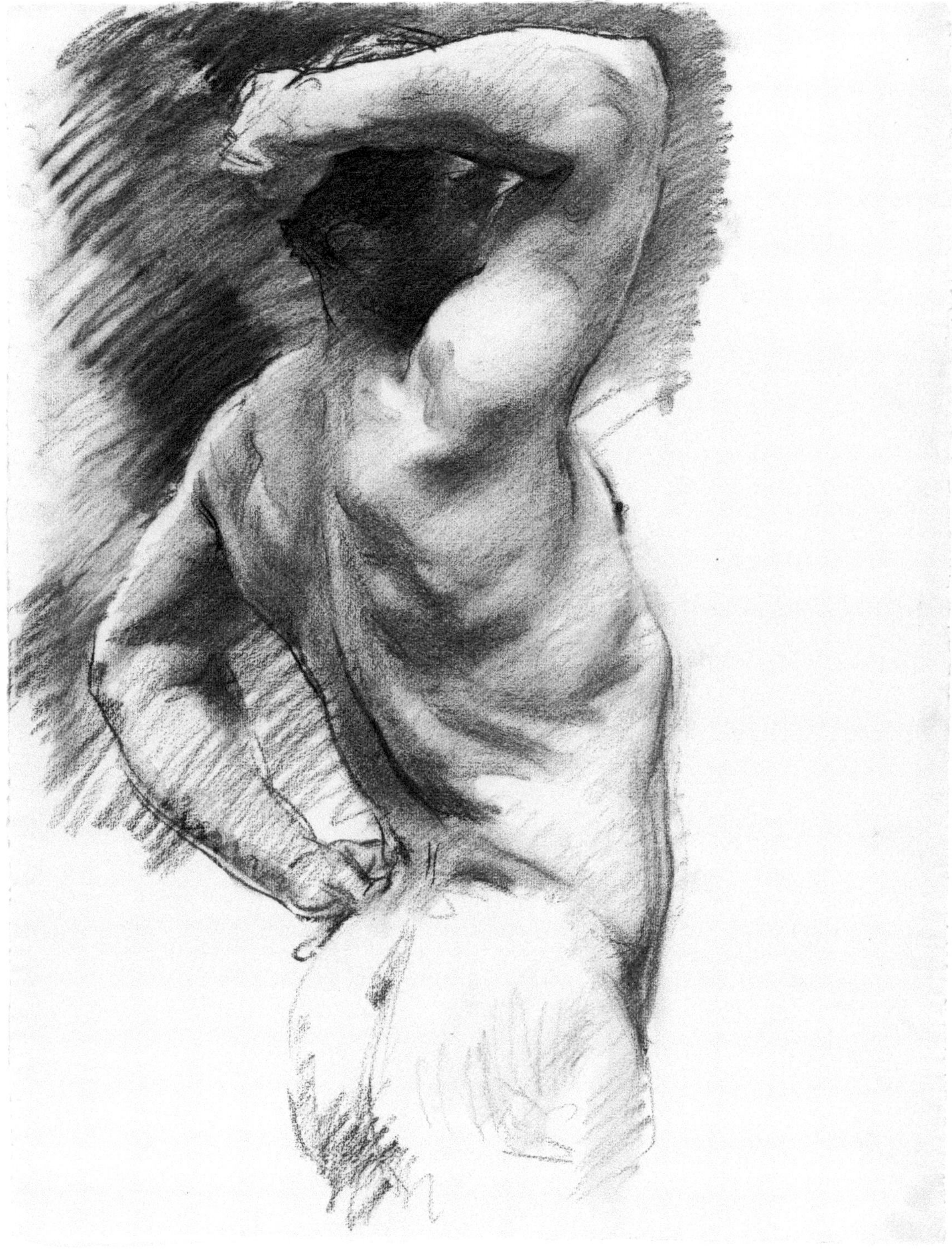

Standing Male Nude with Raised Arms c. 1890–1915

Charcoal on faded blue laid paper, 24 × 18⅝16 inches

Harvard Art Museums/Fogg Museum, Gift of Mrs. Francis Ormond

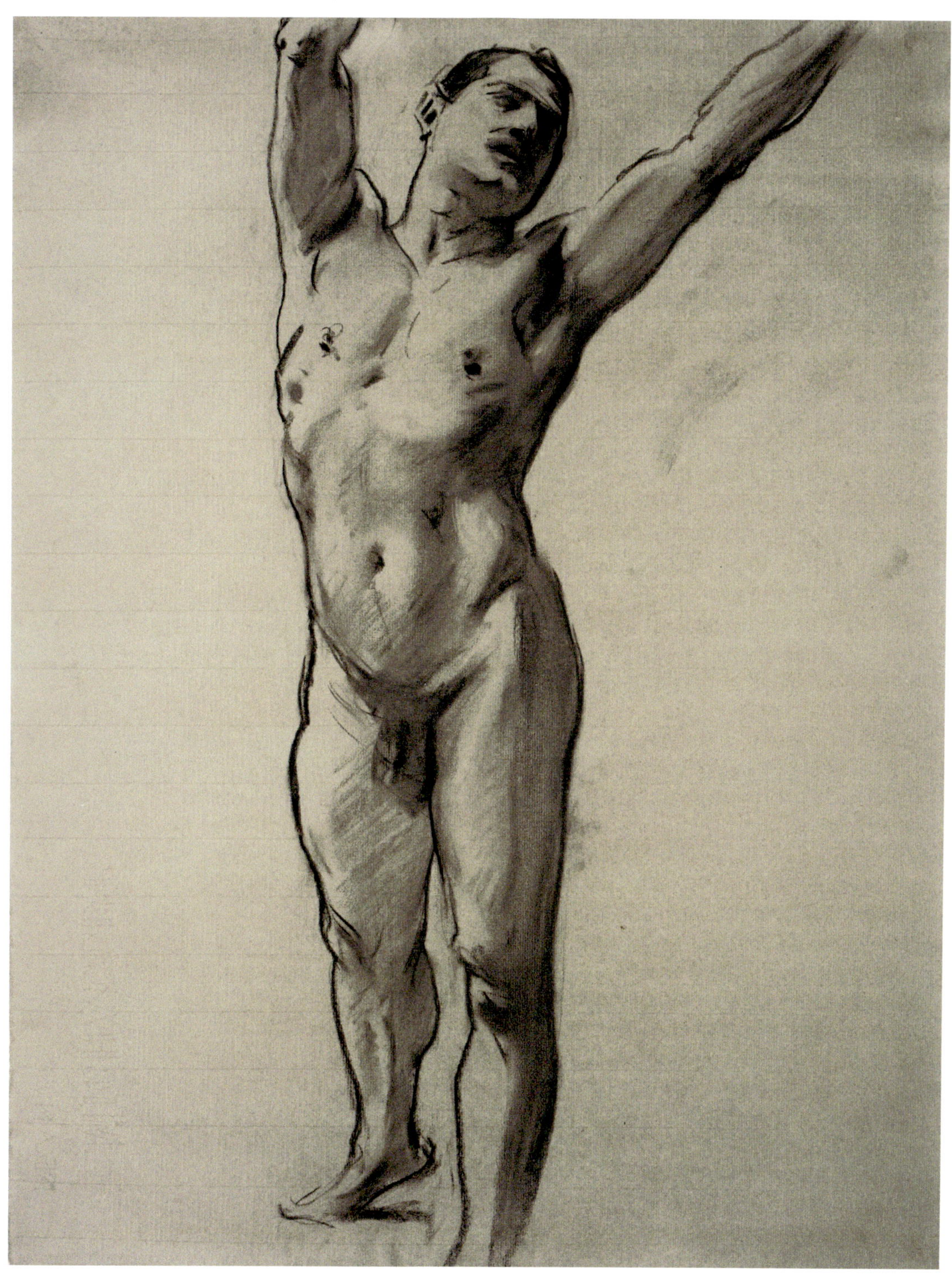

Life Study (Study of an Egyptian Girl) 1891

Oil on canvas, 75 × 24 inches

The Art Institute of Chicago / Art Resource

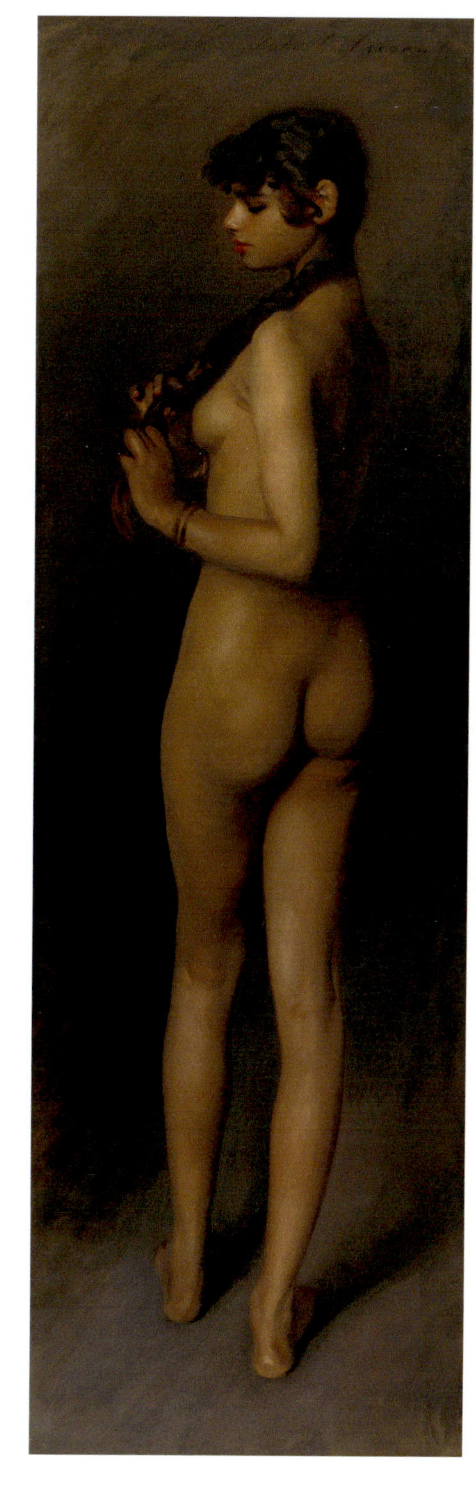

Partial View of a Standing Male Nude c. 1890–1915

Charcoal on off-white laid paper, 24½ × 18$^{9}/_{16}$ inches

Harvard Art Museums/Fogg Museum, Gift of Mrs. Francis Ormond

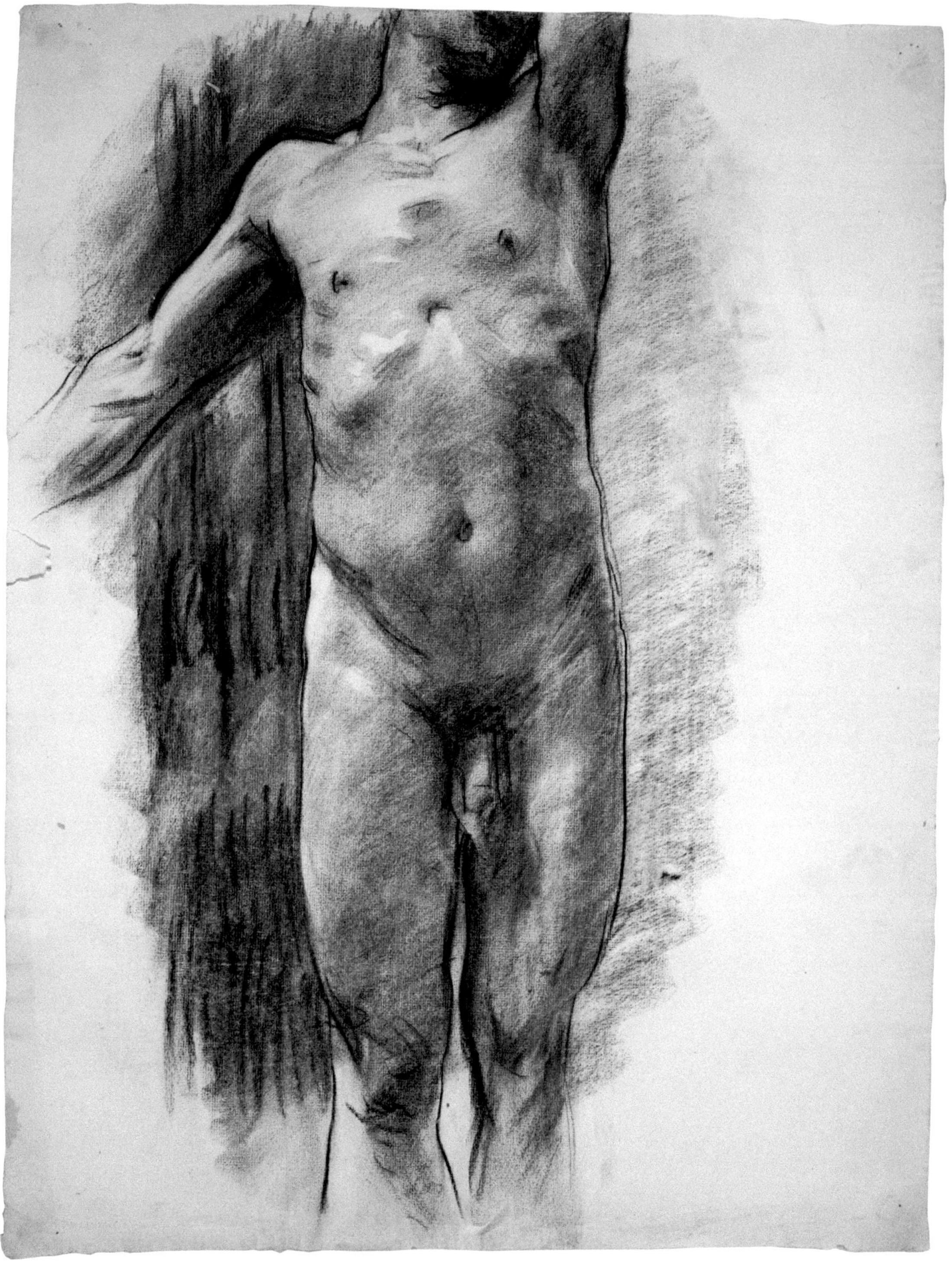

W. Graham Robertson 1894

Oil on canvas, 90¾ × 46¾ inches

Tate, Presented by W. Graham Robertson 1940

Photograph: Tate

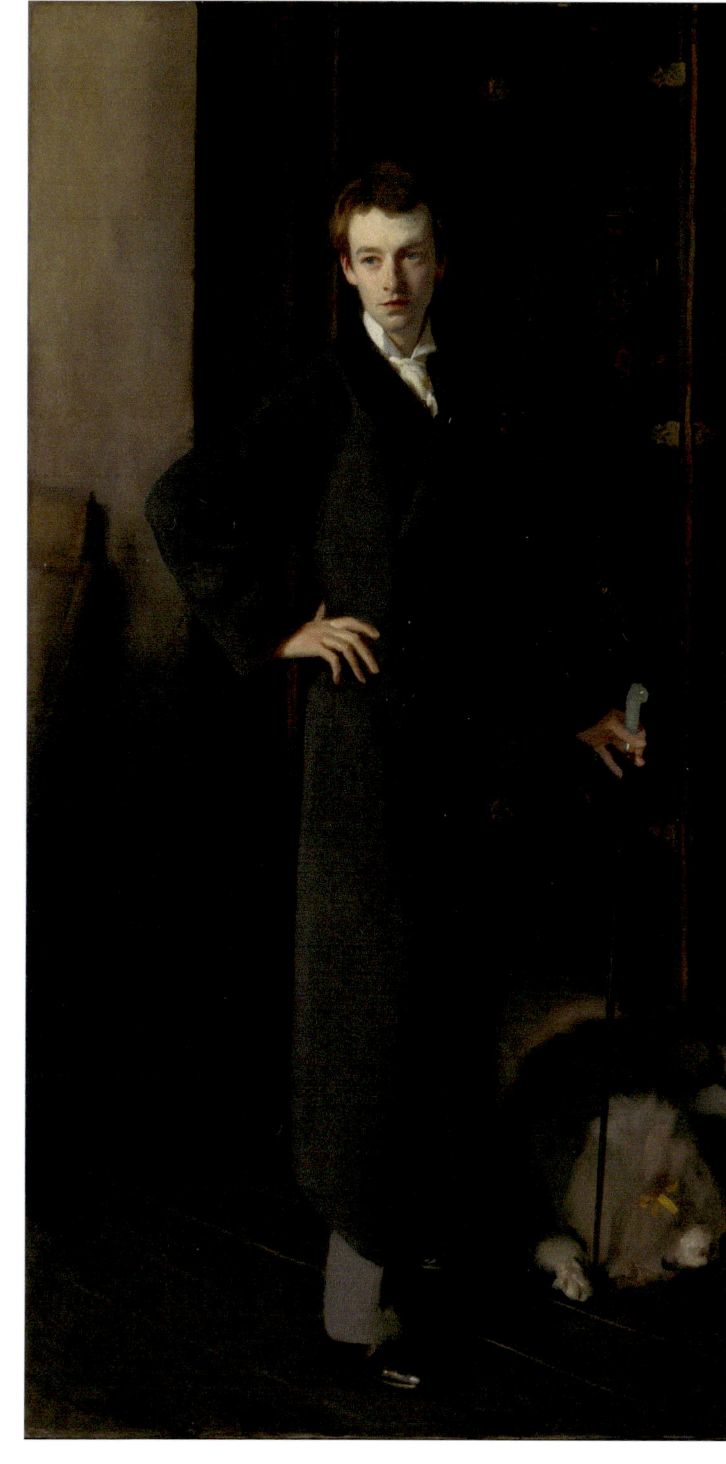

Ena and Betty, Daughters of Asher and Mrs. Wertheimer 1901

Oil on canvas, 75 × 51½ inches

Tate, Presented by the widow and family of Asher Wertheimer in accordance with his wishes 1922

Photograph: Tate

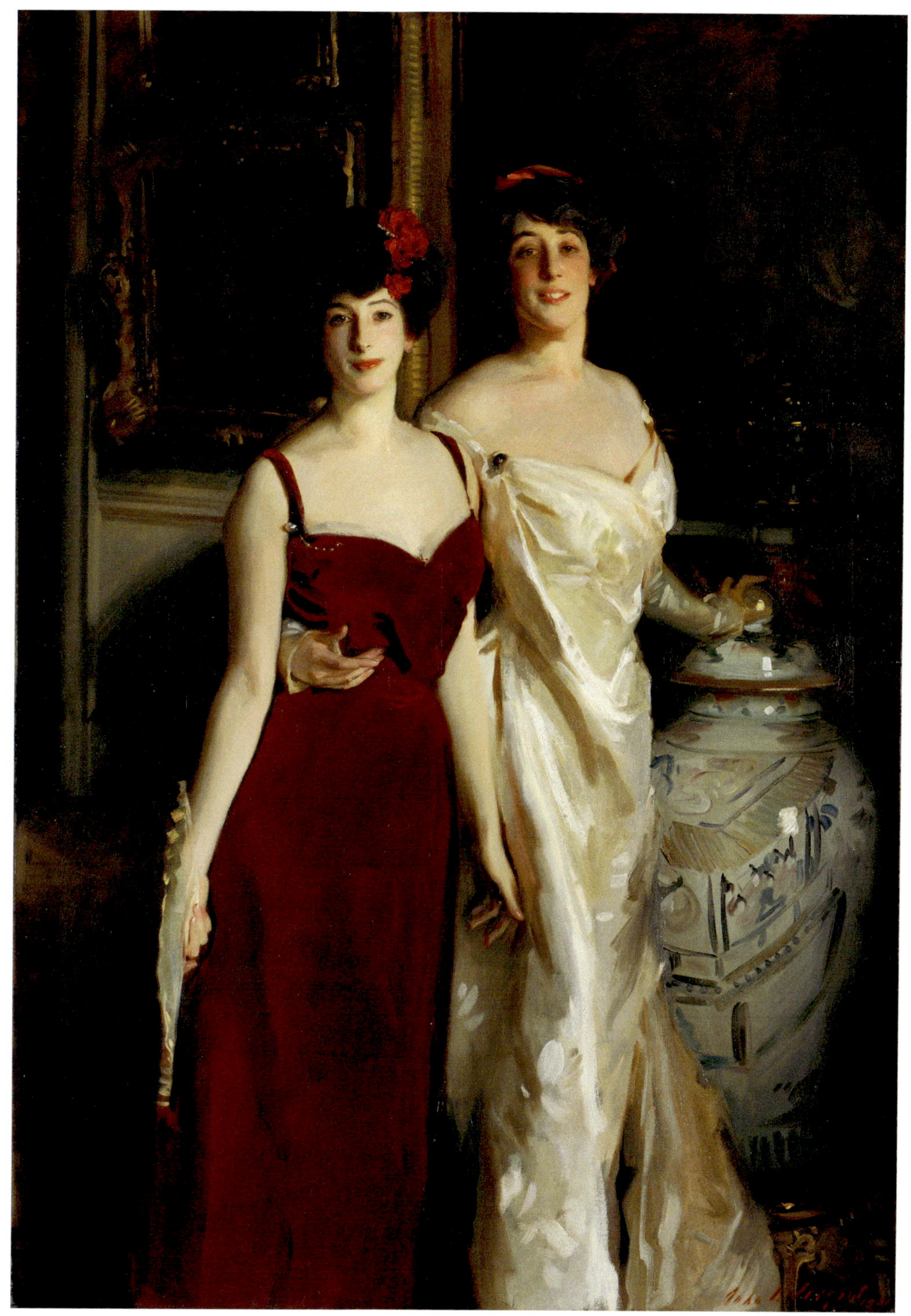

Camping Near Lake O'Hara 1916

Watercolor on paper, 15⅜ × 21 inches

Purchase 1957 Felix Fuld Bequest Fund 57.86

Collection of the Newark Museum of Art

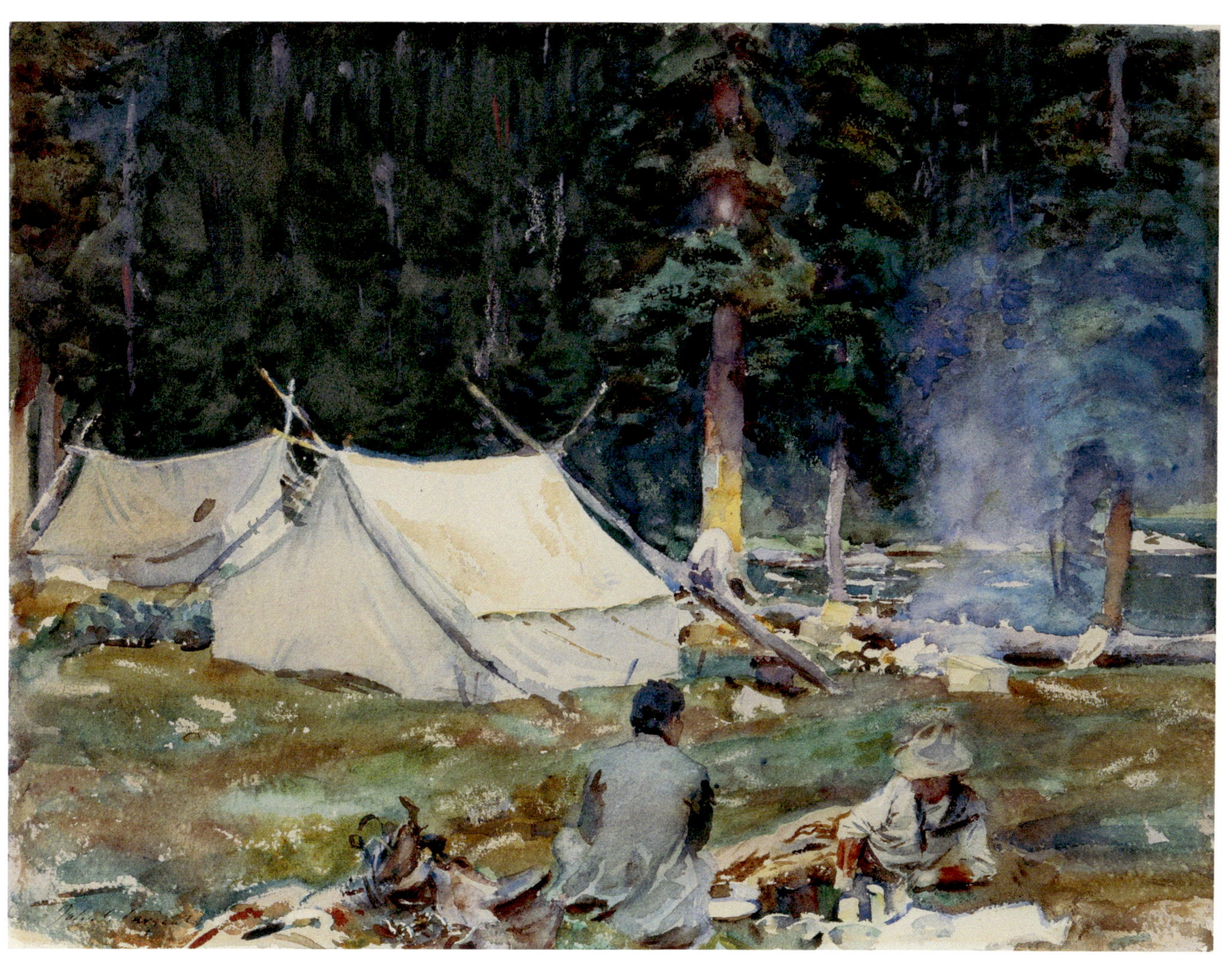

A Tent in the Rockies 1916

Watercolor on paper, 14 15/16 × 20½ inches

Isabella Stewart Gardner Museum, Boston

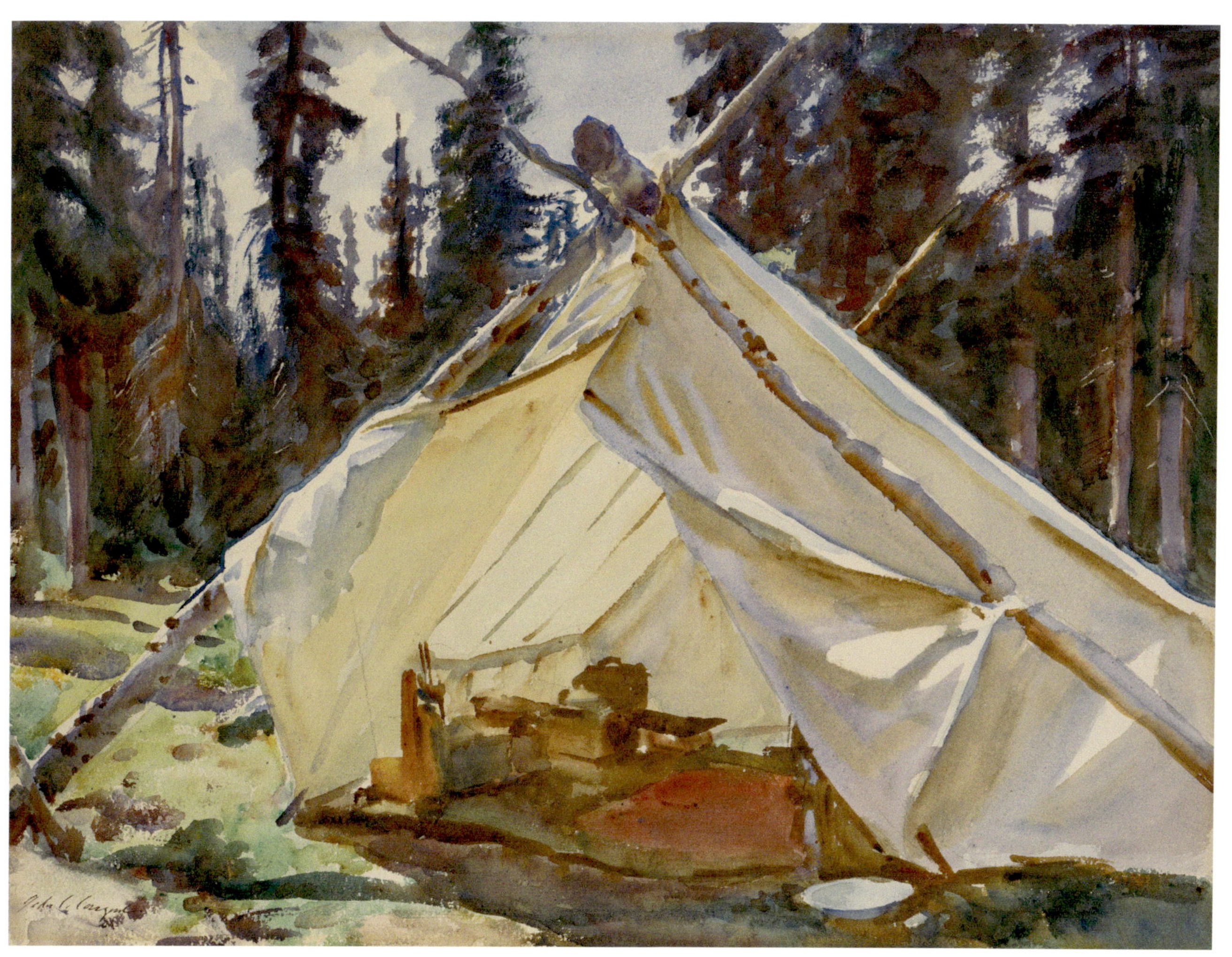

Woman Reclining 1908

Watercolor on paper, 20½ × 37 inches

Cincinnati Art Museum, Ohio, USA

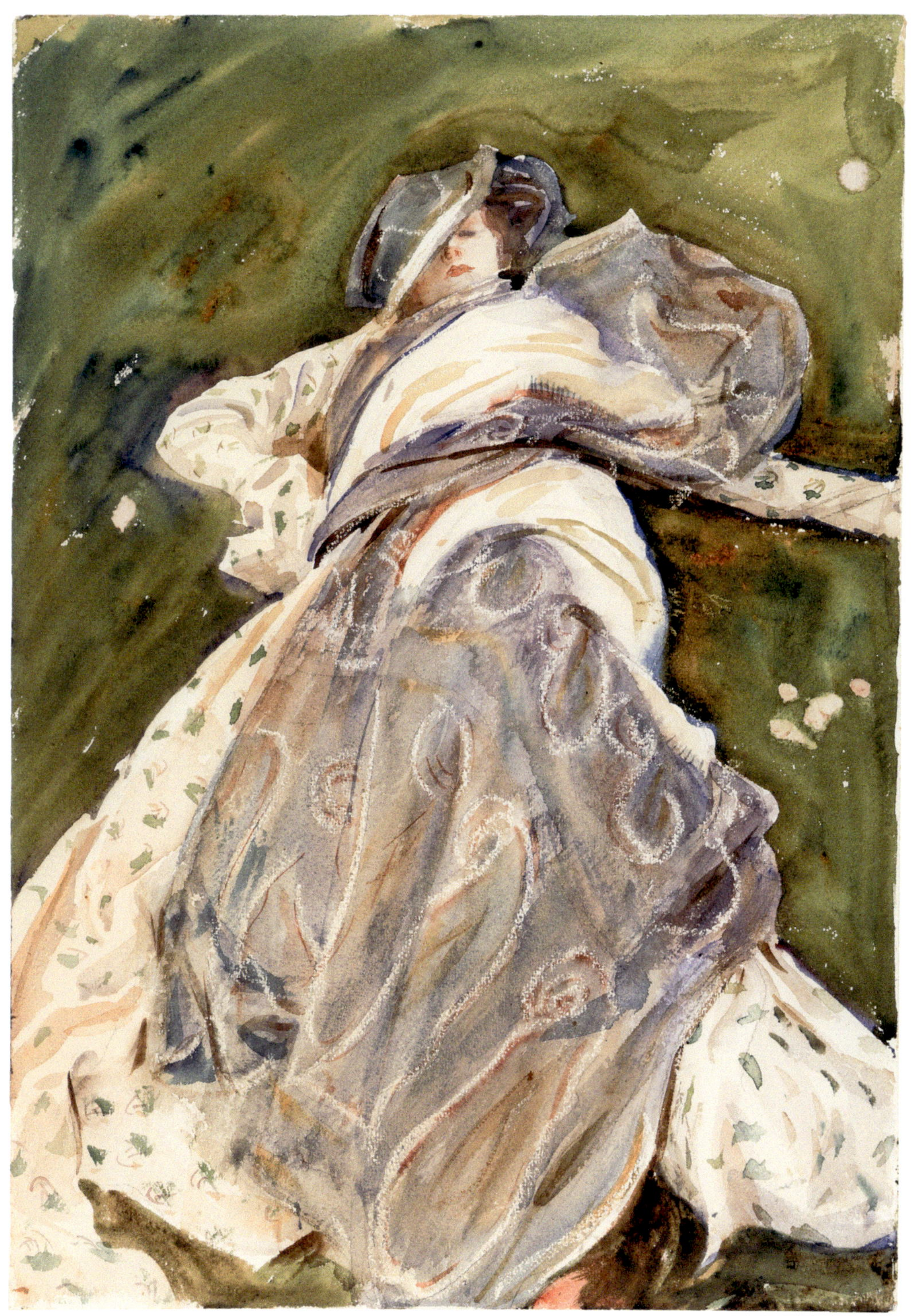

Val d'Aosta: A Man Fishing c. 1907

22¼ × 28¼ inches, Oil on canvas

Addison Gallery of American Art, Phillips Academy, Andover, MA

Gift of anonymous donor / Art Resource, NY

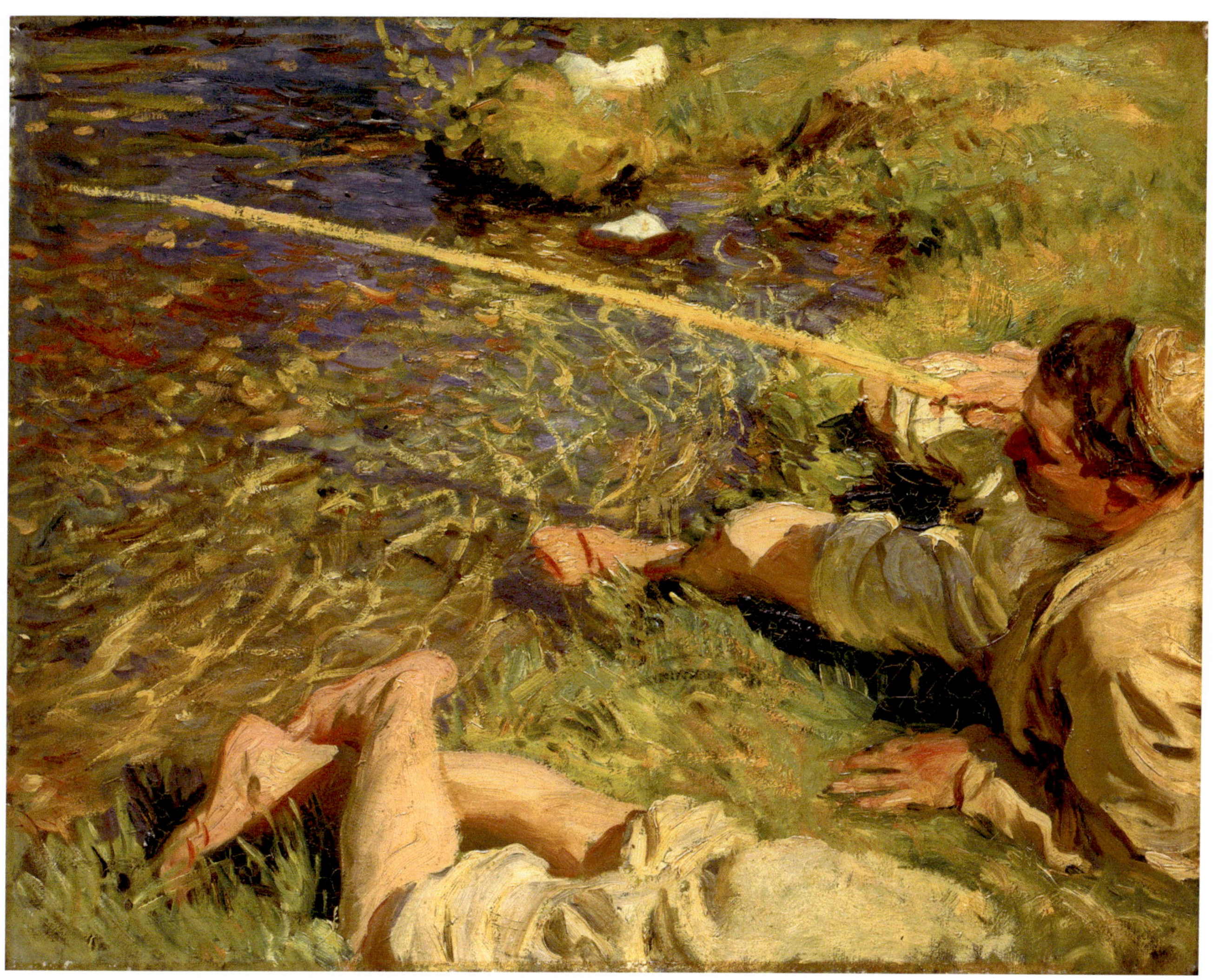

Figure Study c. 1900

Watercolor and pencil on paper, 19 × 21 inches

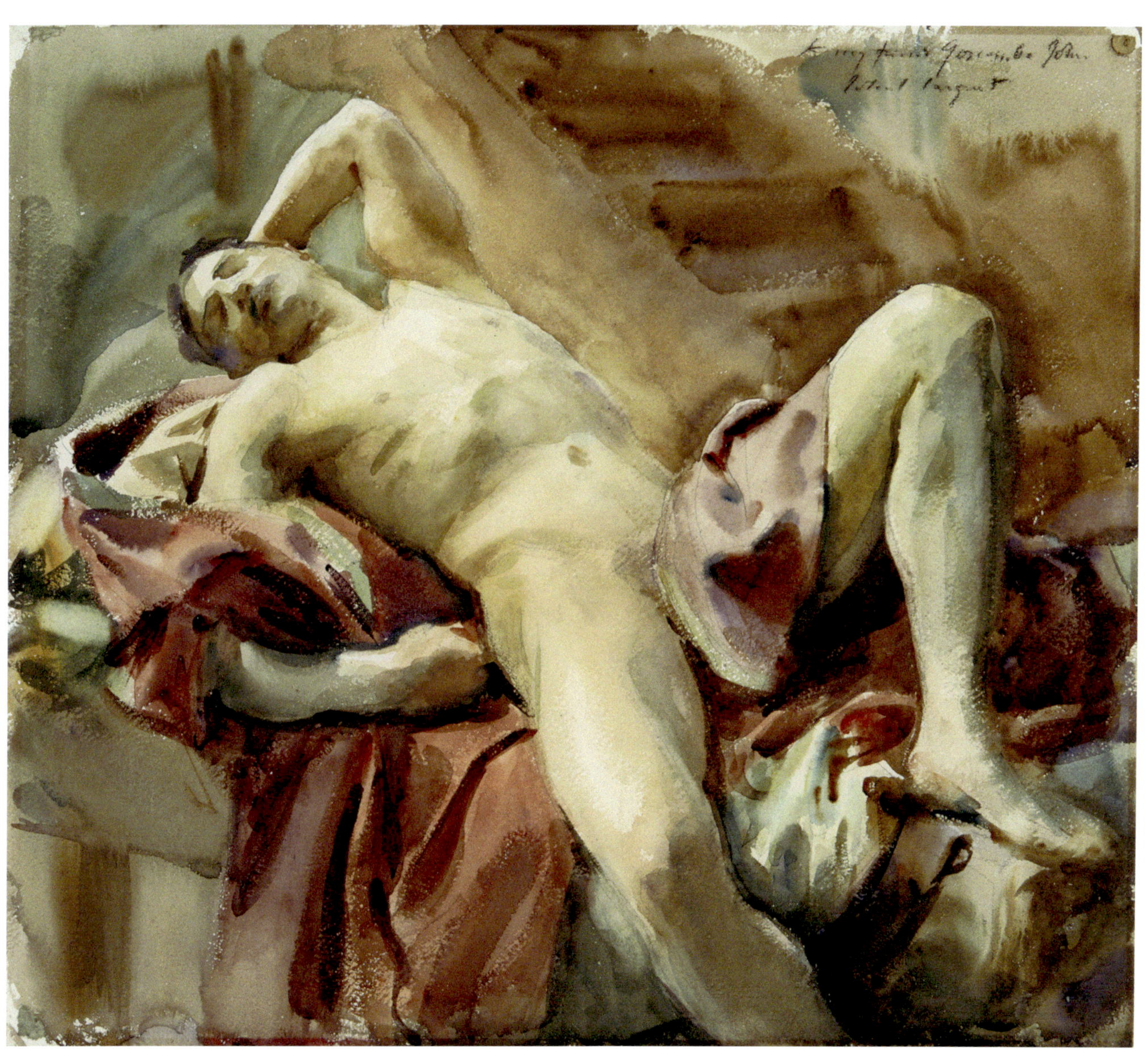

Study of a Male Nude Reclining c. 1904

Watercolor and pencil on paper, 38 × 22 inches

UCL Art Museum, University College London, UK

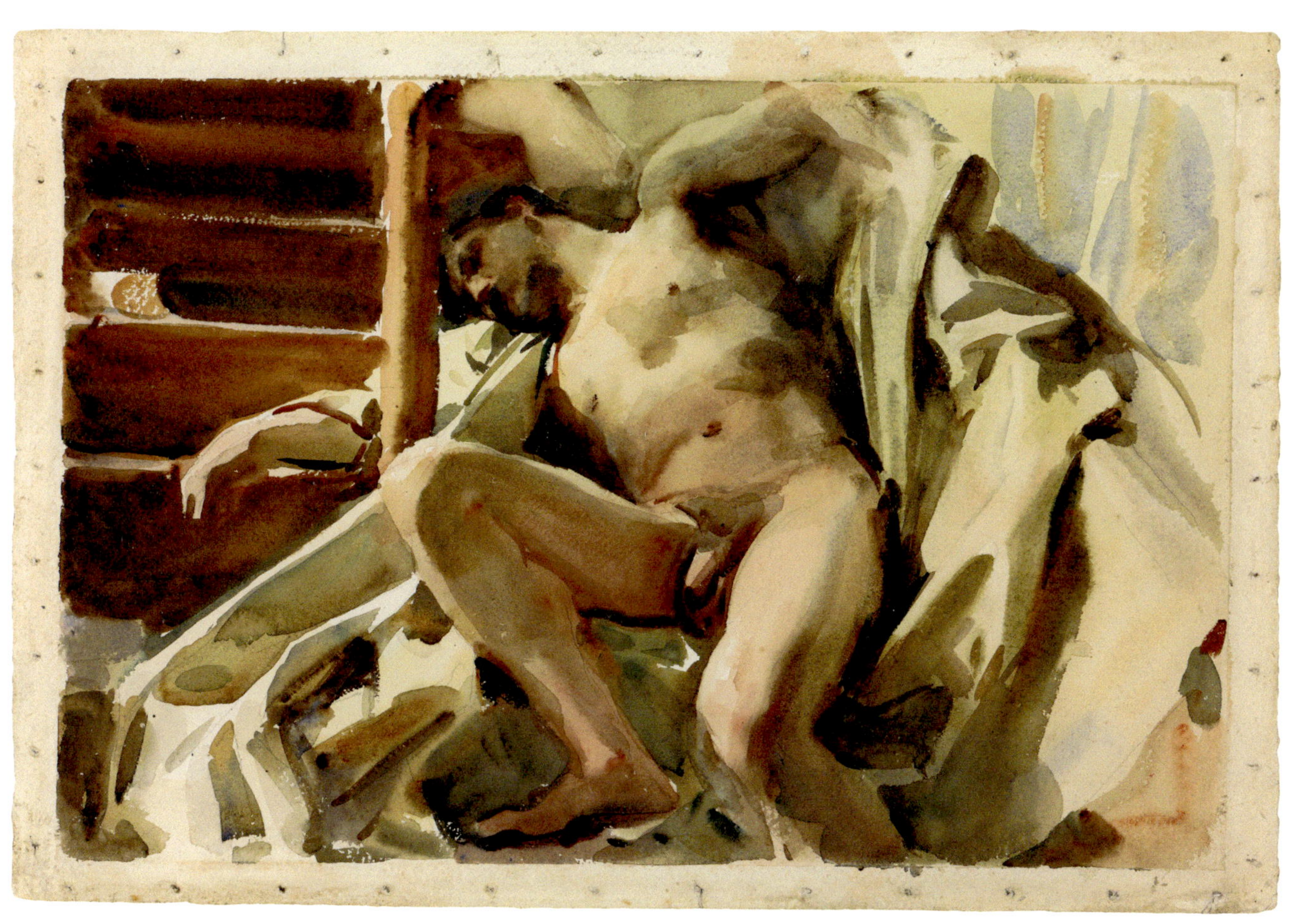

Fumée d'ambre gris (Smoke of Ambergris) 1880

Oil on canvas, 54⅗ × 35¹¹⁄₁₆ inches

Image courtesy of Clark Art Institute

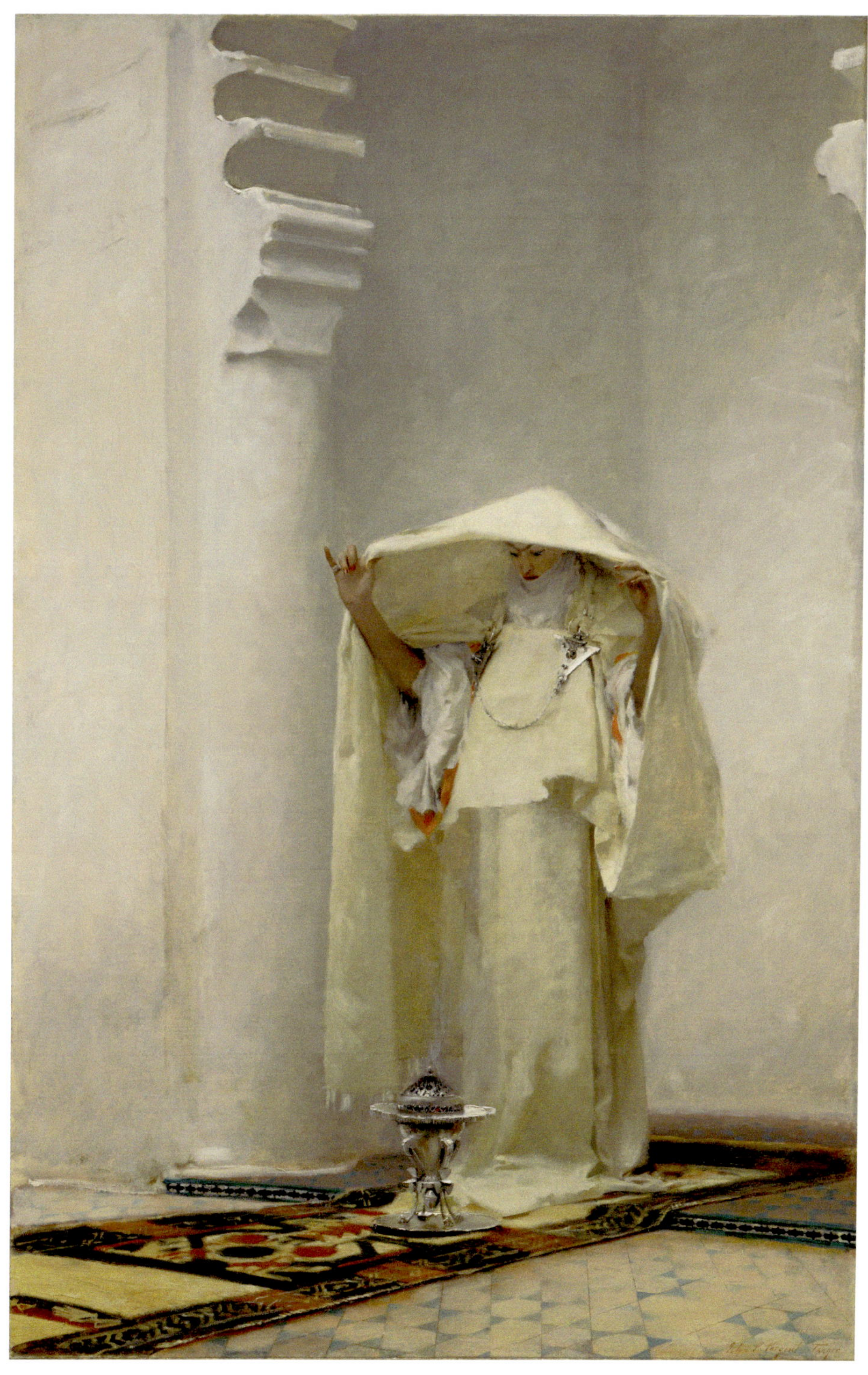

The Bridge of Sighs c. 1903–1904
Translucent and opaque watercolor with graphite and red-pigmented underdrawing, 10 × 14 inches
Brooklyn Museum, Purchased by Special Subscription, 09.819

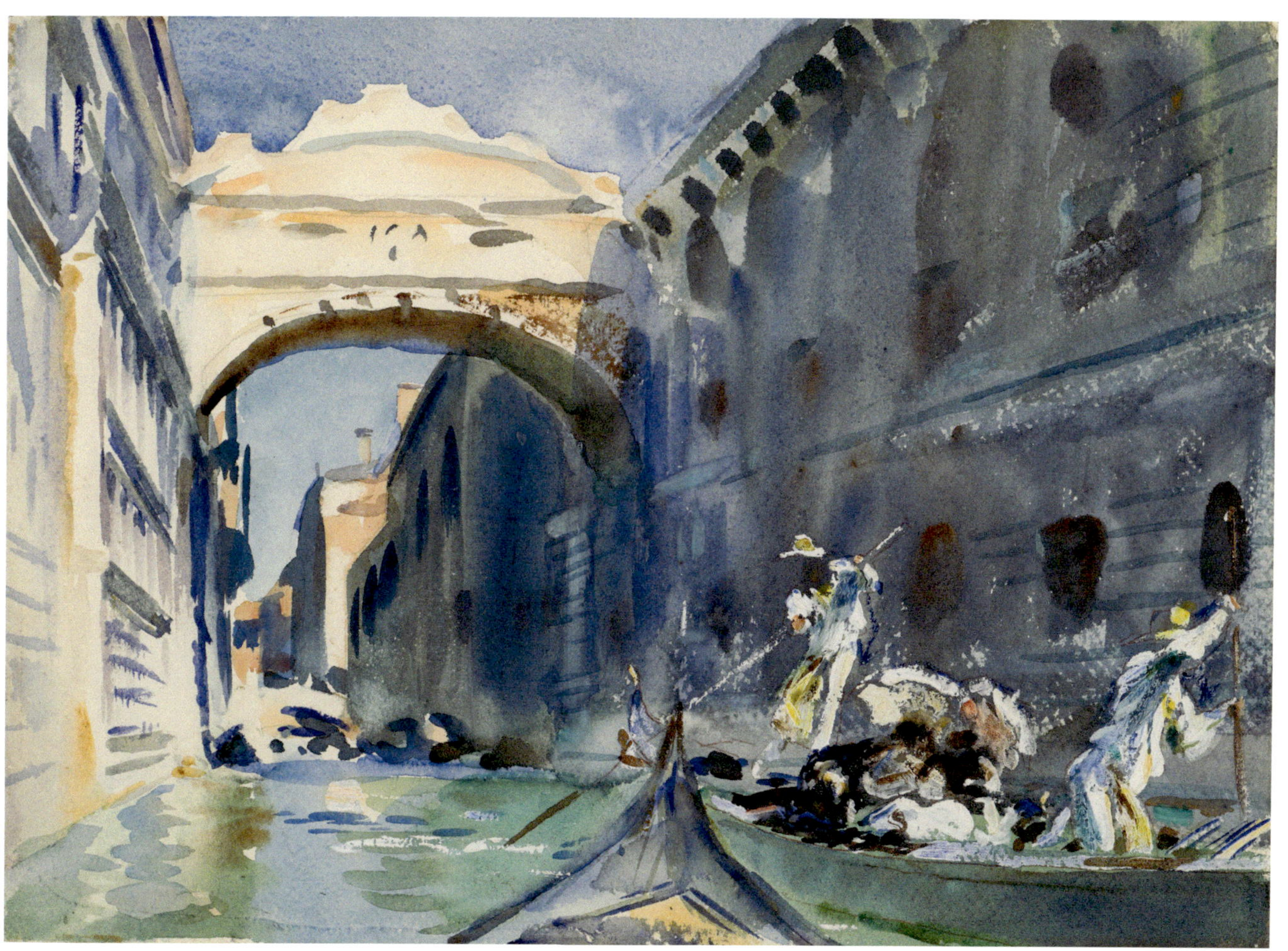

Man and Pool, Florida 1917

Watercolor, gouache, and graphite on white wove paper, 13 11/16 × 21 inches

The Metropolitan Museum of Art, Gift of Francis Ormond

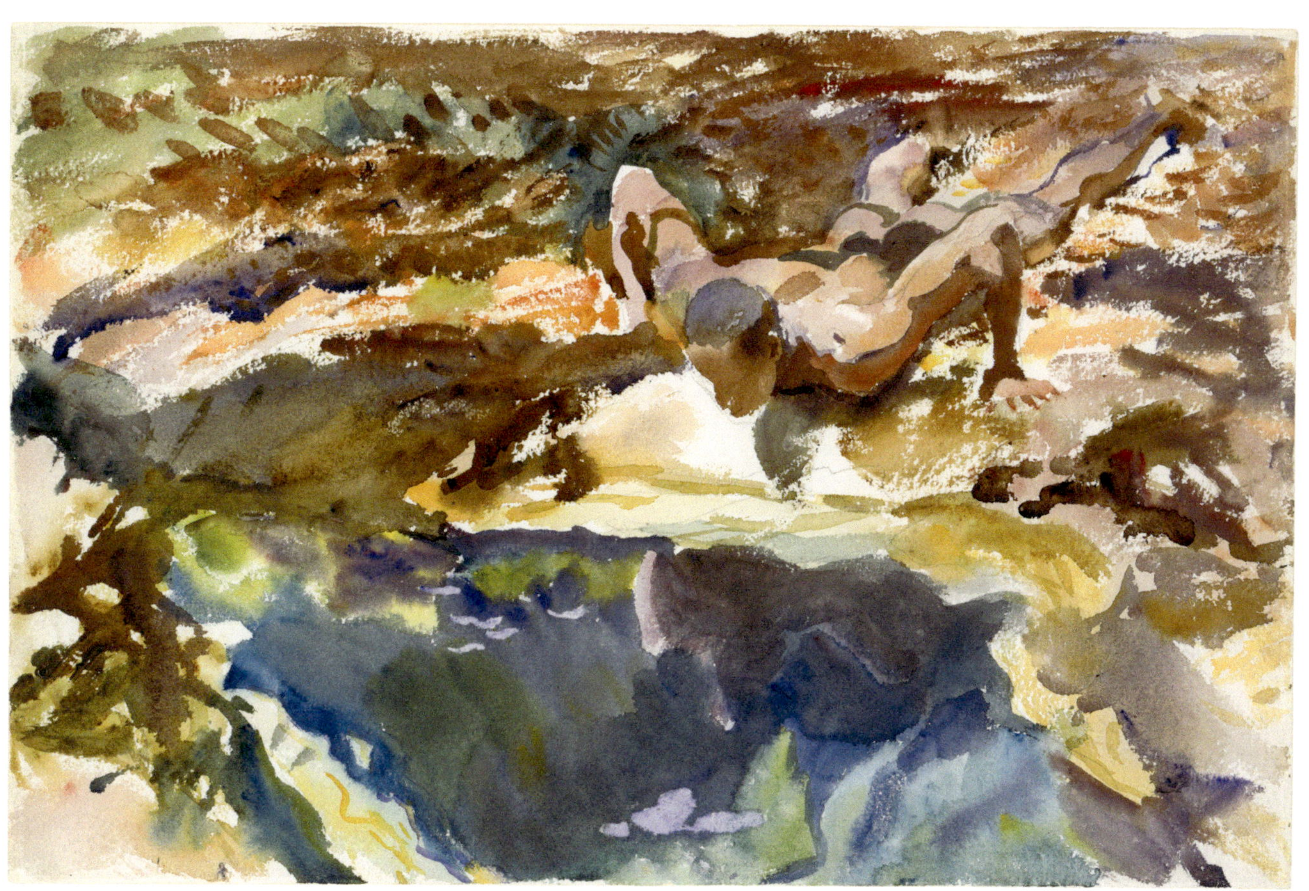

The Parting of Jonathan and David c. 1895

Charcoal on off-white laid paper

23⅝ × 17¹³⁄₁₆ inches

Harvard Art Museums/Fogg Museum, Gift of Mrs. Francis Ormond

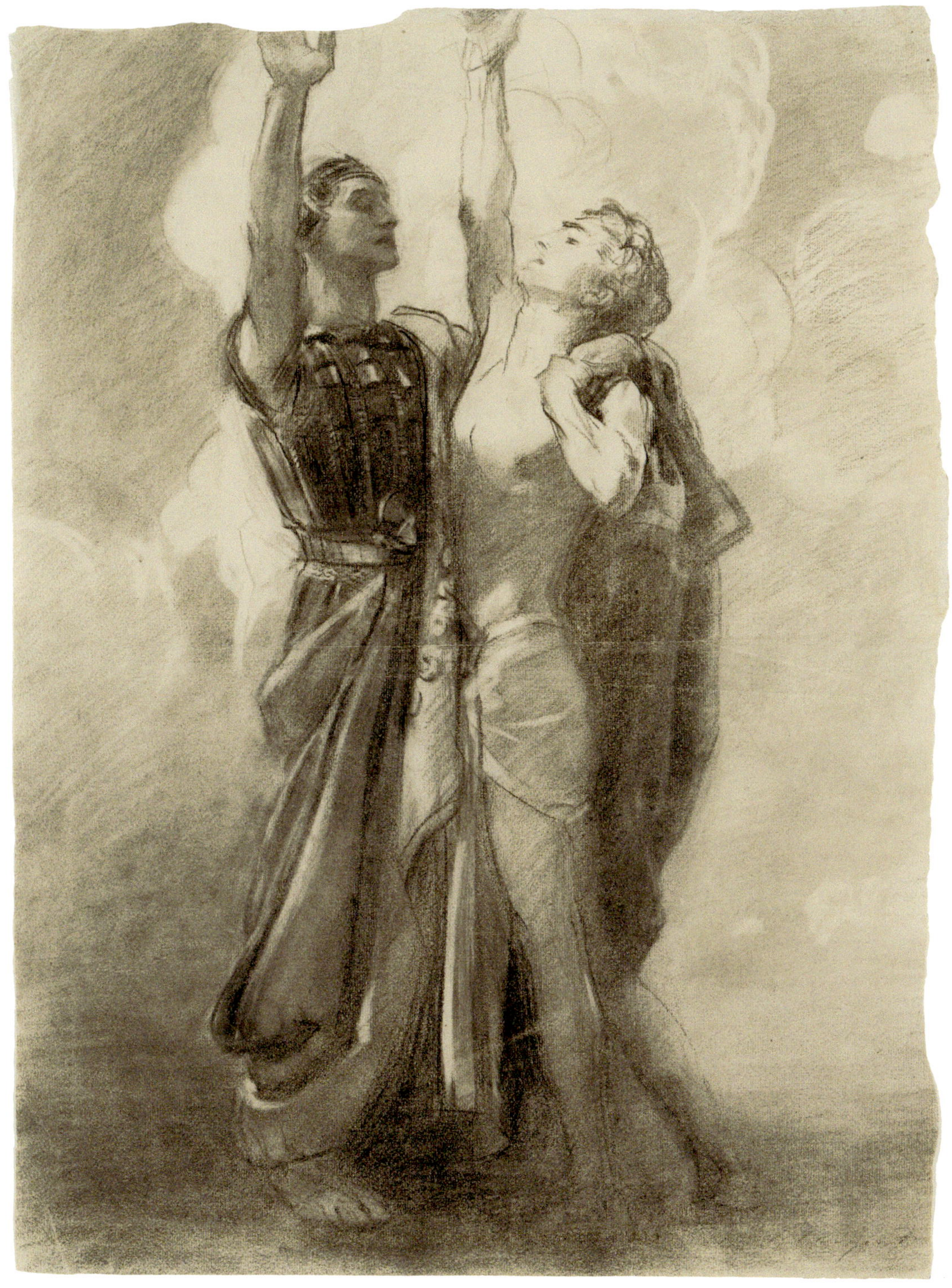

Study for "Prometheus," Museum of Fine Arts, Boston 1916–1921
Oil on canvas, 45 × 45 inches
Harvard Art Museums / Fogg Museum, Transfer from
the Harvard University Graduate School of Design
(assumed to be a Gift of Emily Sargent and Violet Ormond
in memory of their brother, John Singer Sargent)
Photograph © President and Fellows of Harvard College, 1994.169

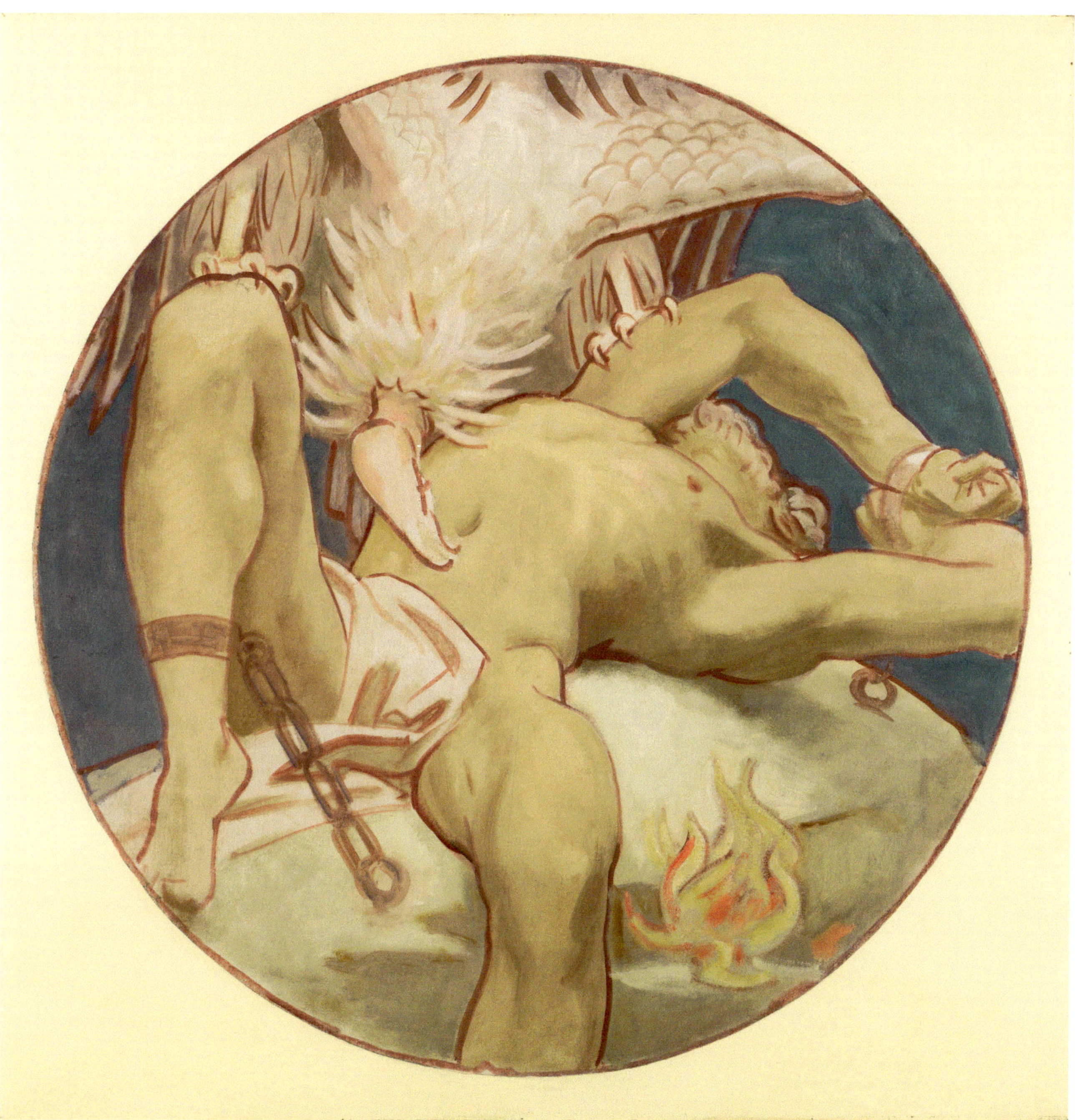

Nude Study of Thomas E. McKeller 1917–1920

Oil on canvas, 49½ × 33¼ inches

Museum of Fine Arts, Boston,

Henry H. and Zoe Oliver Sherman Fund

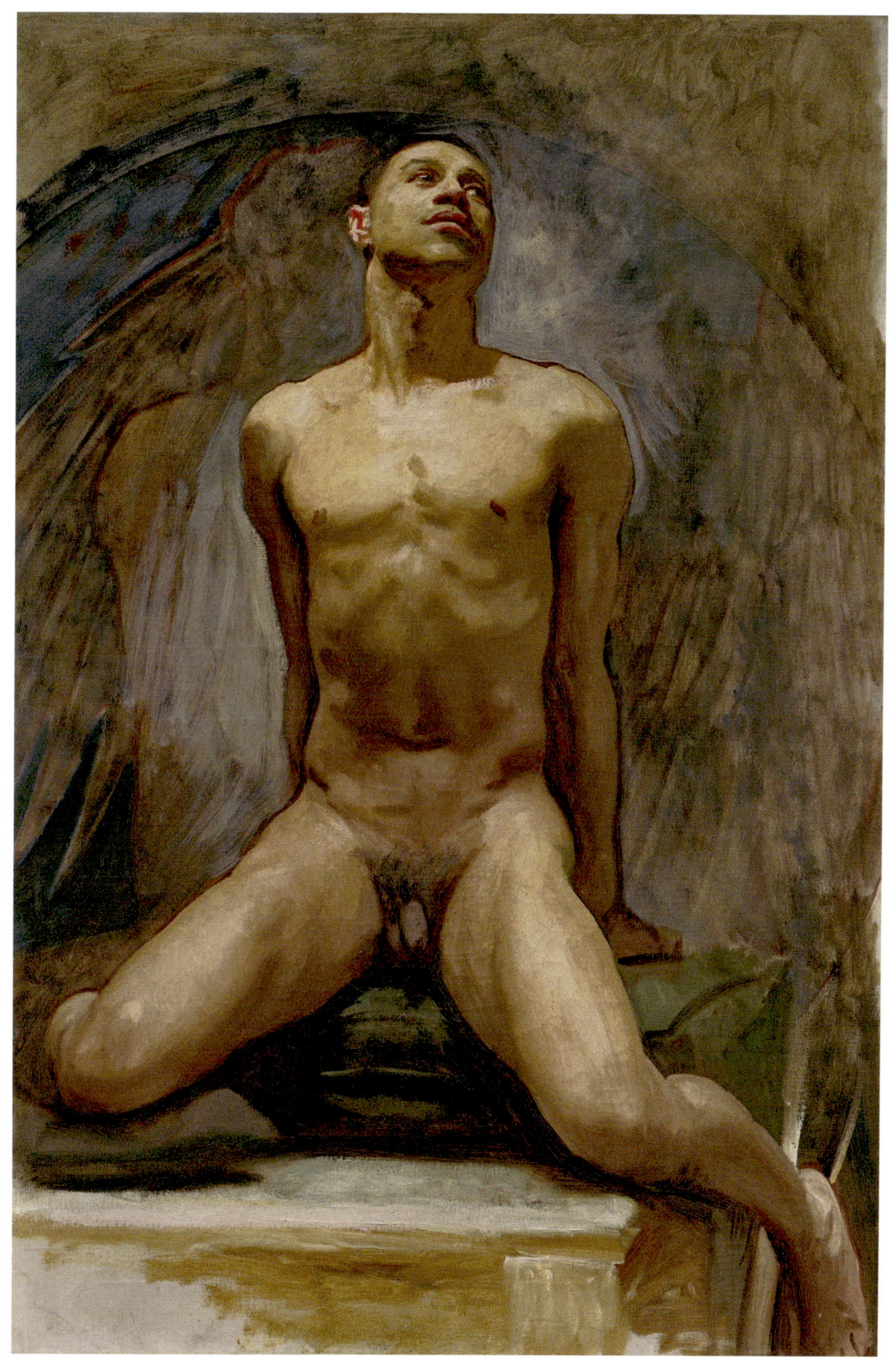

Tommies Bathing 1918

Watercolor and graphite on white wove paper, 15⅝⁄16 × 20¾ inches

The Metropolitan Museum of Art, Gift of Mrs. Francis Ormond, 1950

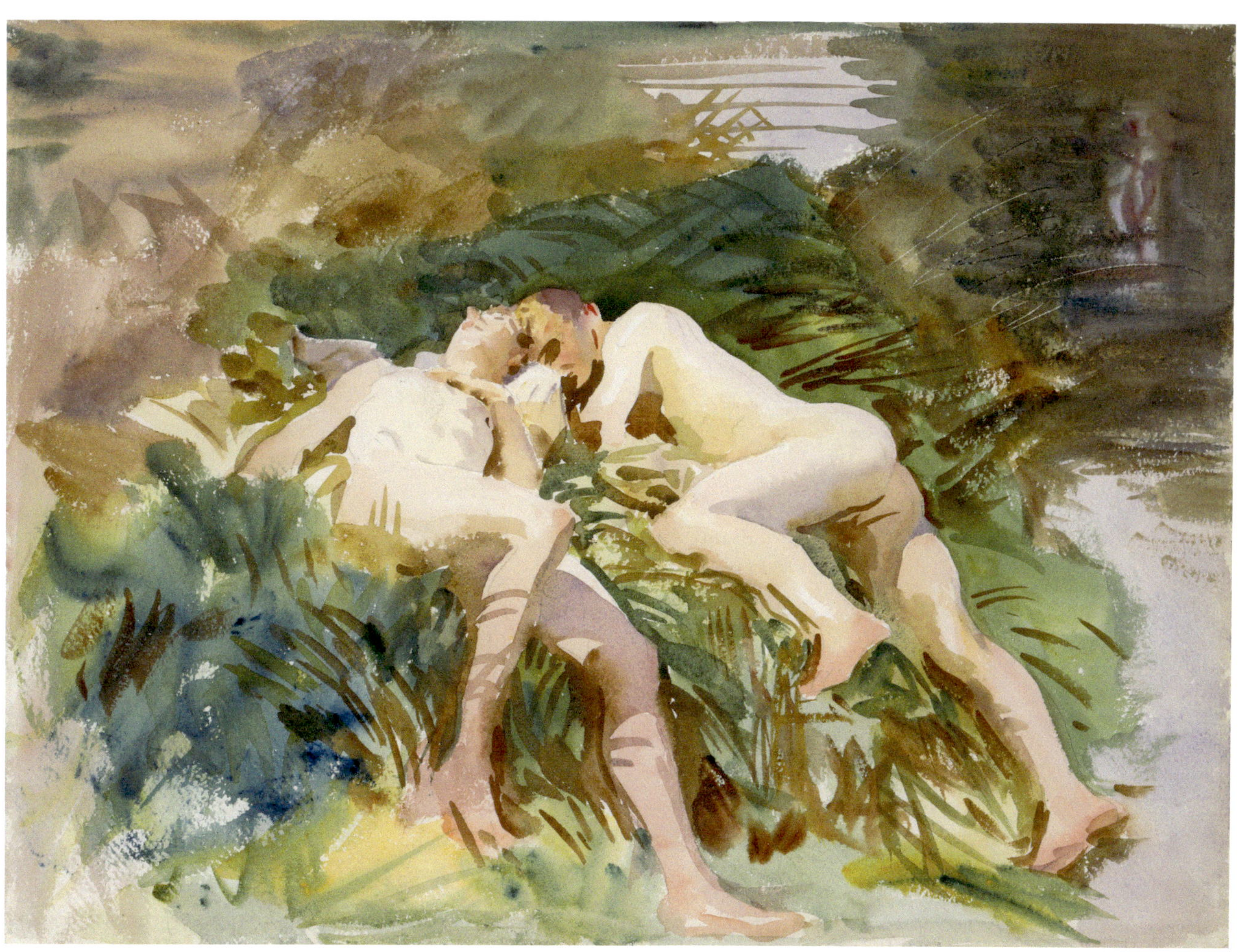

"Thou Shalt Not Steal" 1918

Watercolor on paper, 34 × 26½

IWC. Art.IWM ART 1609

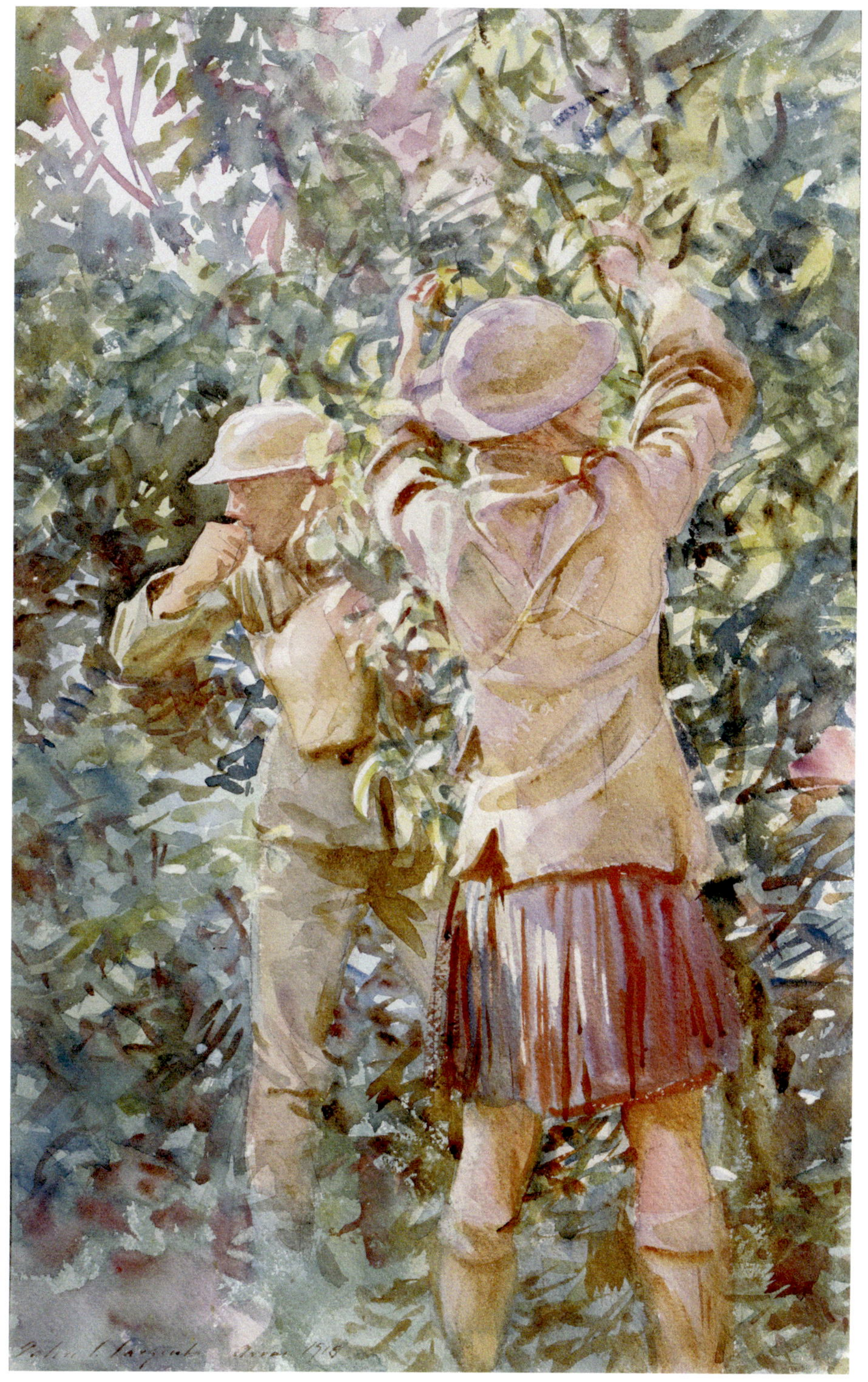

Reclining Male Nude c. 1890–1915

Charcoal on off-white laid paper, 18⅝ × 24⅝ inches

Harvard Art Museums/Fogg Museum, Gift of Mrs. Francis Ormond

Photograph © President and Fellows of Harvard College, 1937.9.7

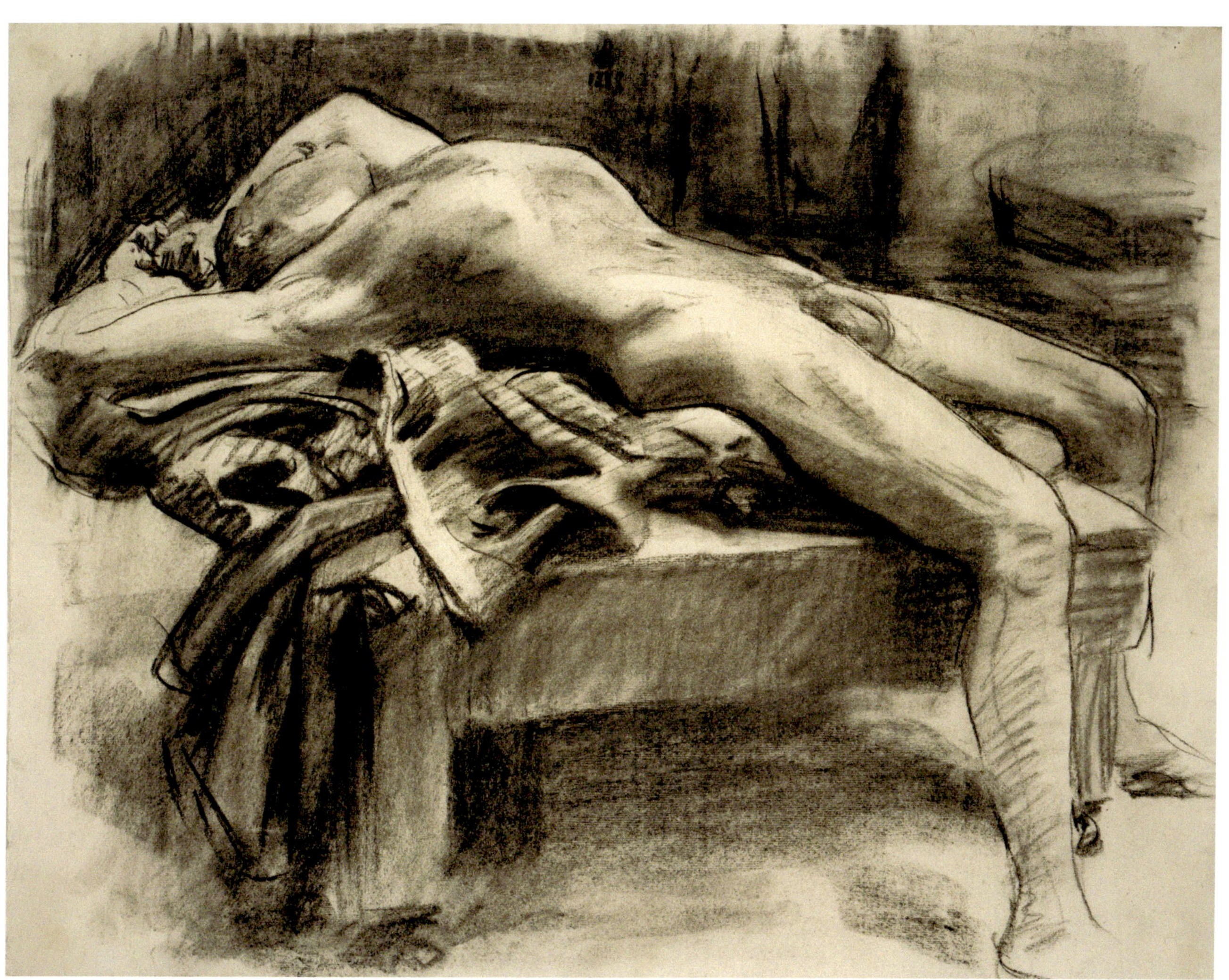

Crescenzo Fusciardi c. 1890–1915

Charcoal on faded blue laid paper, 24 × 18⅝ inches

Harvard Art Museums/Fogg Museum, Gift of Mrs. Francis Ormond

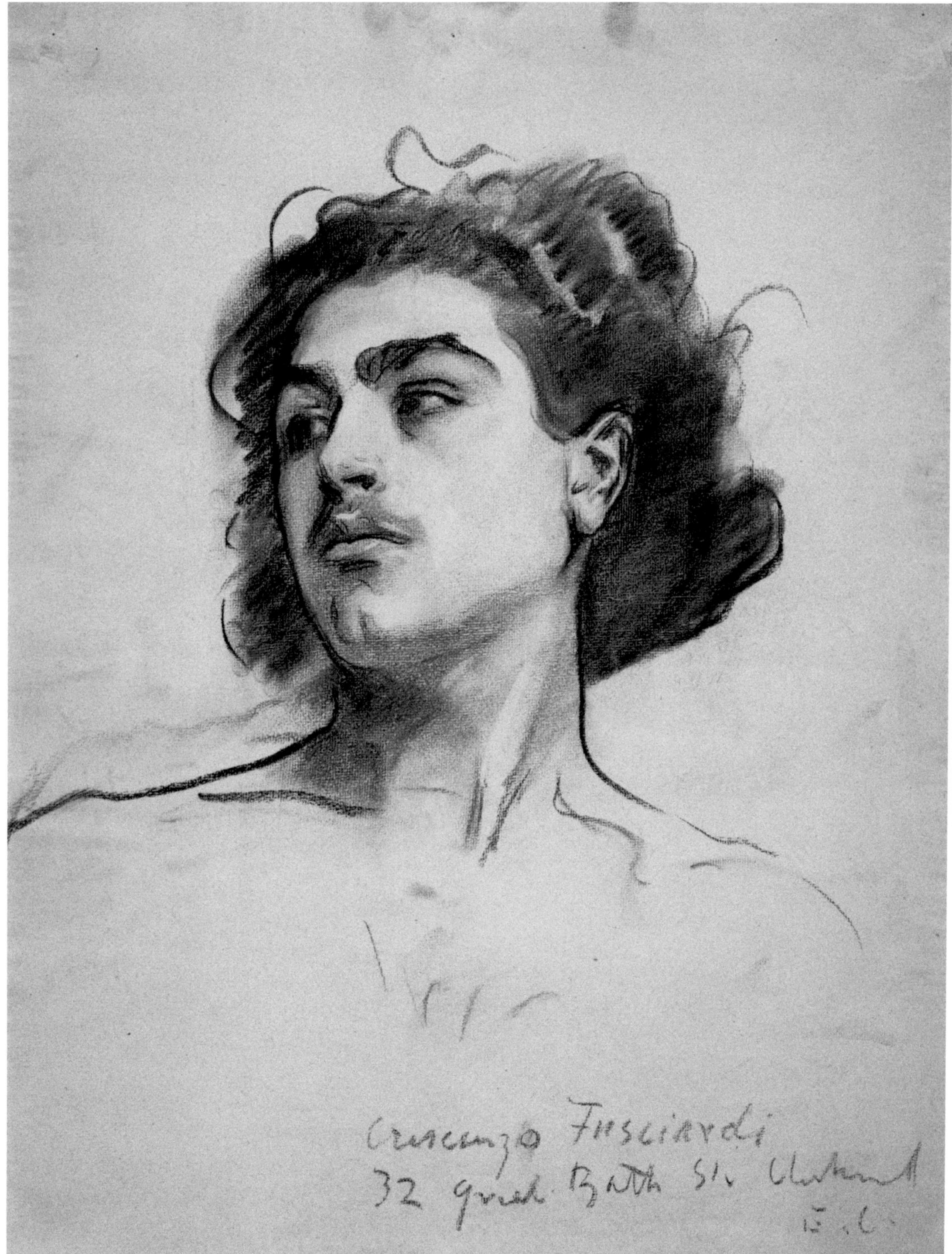
Crescenzo Fusciardi
32 Great Bath St. Clerkenwell
E.C.

Spanish Male Dancer before Nine Seated Figures 1879

Brown ink and brown wash on off-white wove paper, 5¼ × 8⅛ inches

Harvard Art Museums/Fogg Museum, Gift of Mrs. Francis Ormond

Photograph © President and Fellows of Harvard College, 1937.8.2

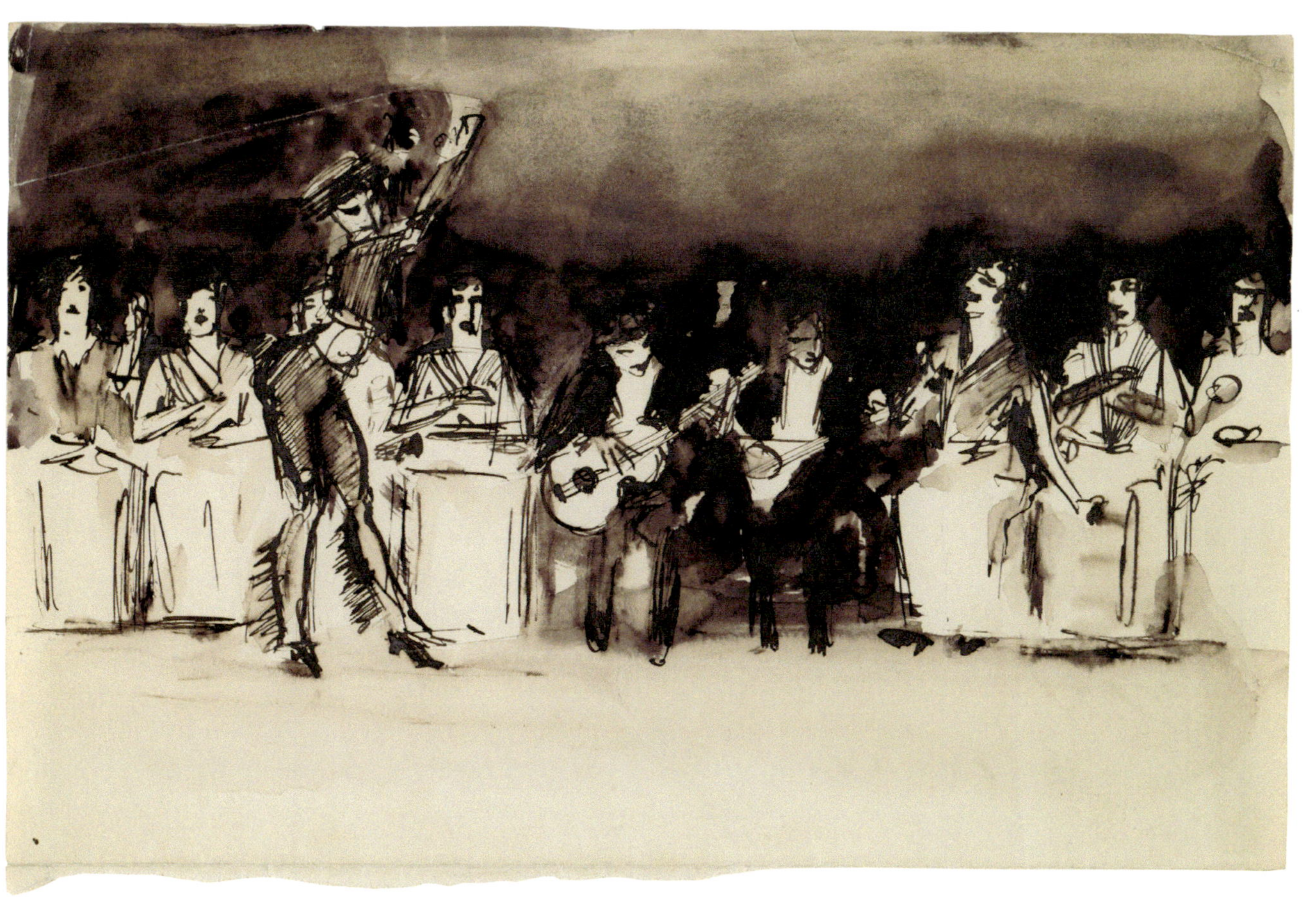

After "El-Jaleo" c. 1882

Graphite and watercolor on prepared clay-coated paper, 10⅛ × 5½ inches

The Metropolitan Museum of Art, Gift of Mrs. Francis Ormond, 1950

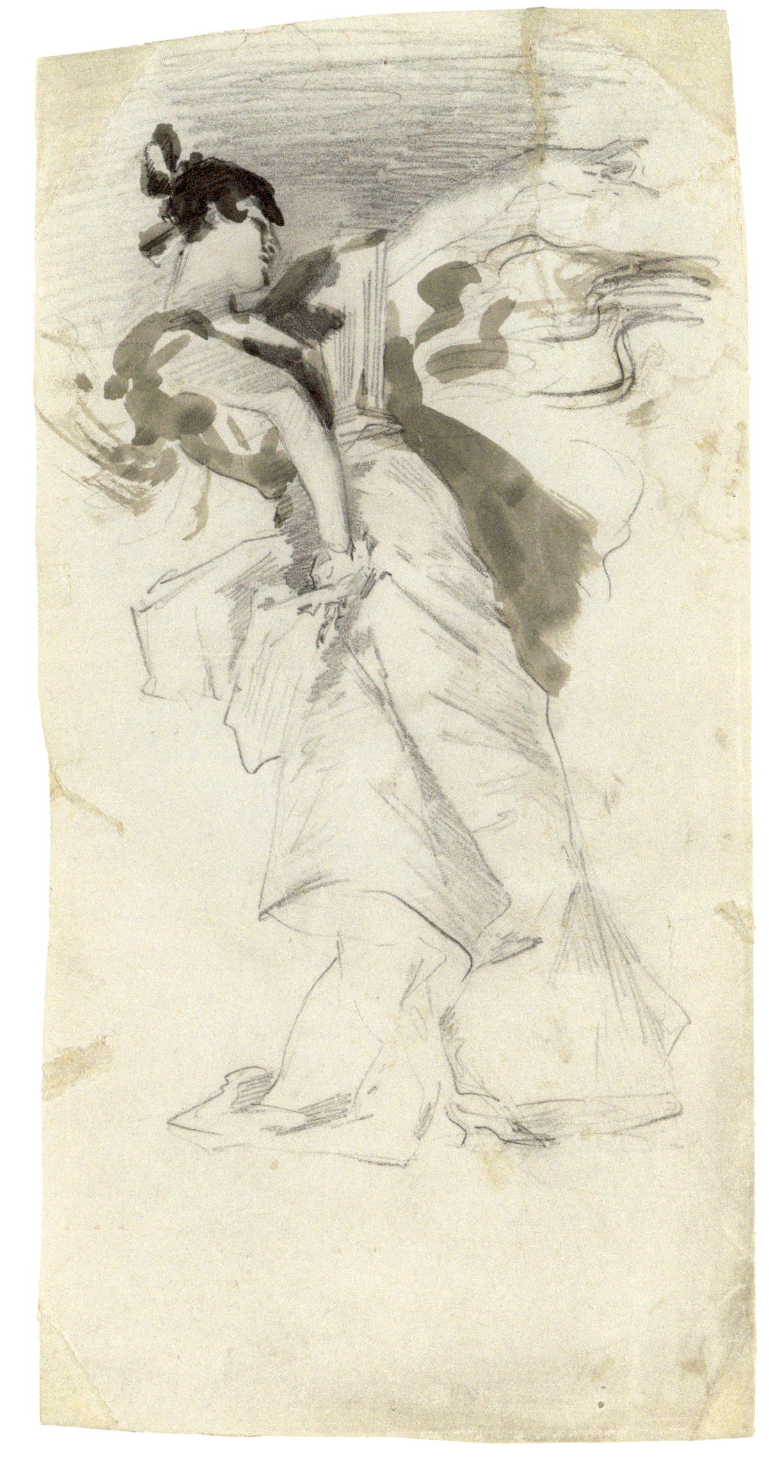

A Male Model, Seated 1909

Oil on canvas, 21 × 17 inches

Private collection

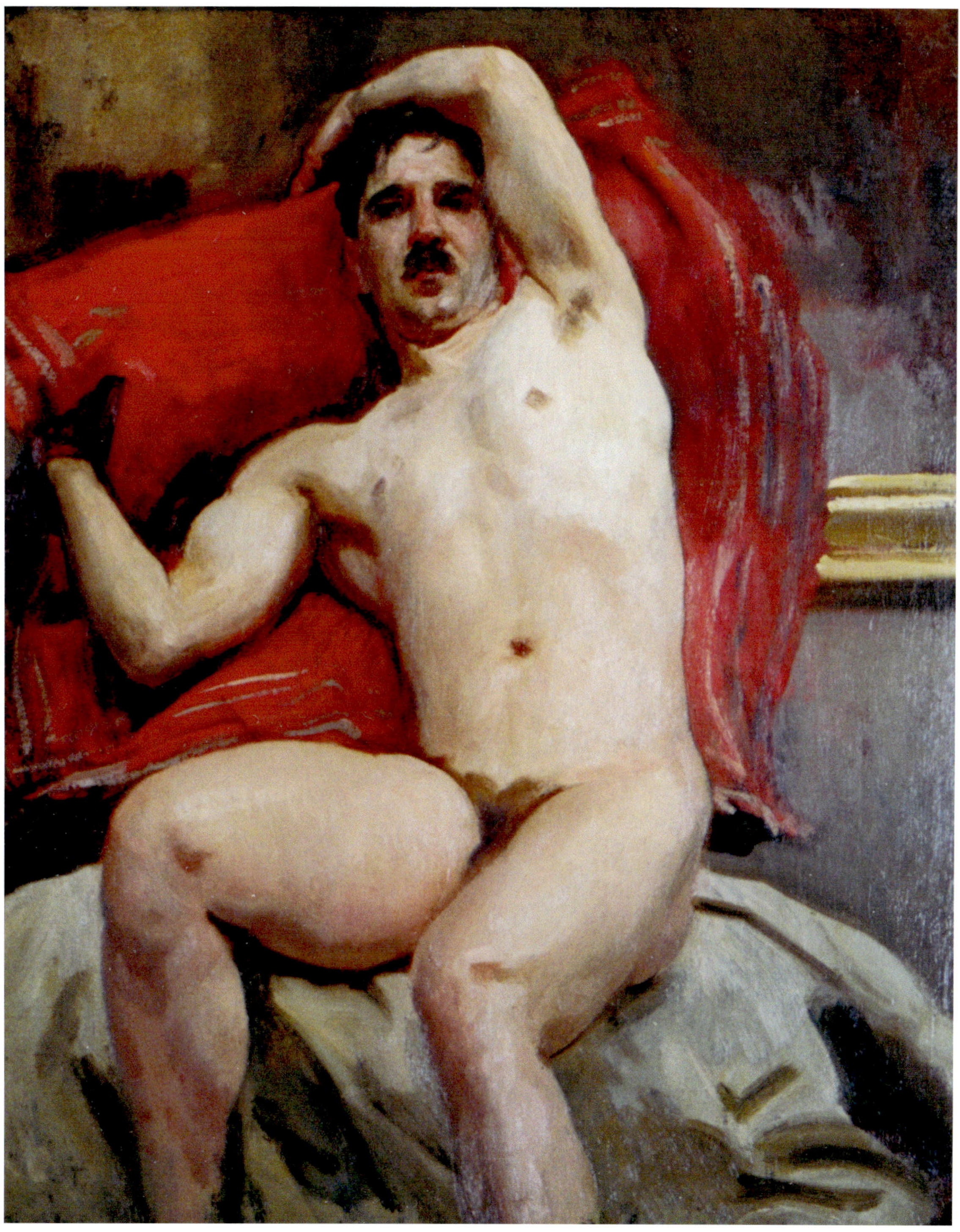

A Conversation

Donald Platt and Trevor Fairbrother

FEBRUARY 2022 – NOVEMBER 2024

DP: We got acquainted in a casual email exchange in 2007 about whether a male nude painted by Sargent was wearing a black glove or not. I had imagined that he was, and you thought it was an awkward shadow the artist hadn't completely worked out.

Tell me about the act of seeing and interpreting as a museum curator.

TF: You had written a curator at the Met, and she passed you on to me, hoping that a gay Sargent scholar would help the person with a question about male nudes! Neither of us had seen the actual painting, and we were responding to color photos from magazines.

I couldn't think of any comparable work by Sargent featuring a glove. His models are naked or partially draped. I don't associate him with the kind of playfulness or eccentricity that would depict a nude wearing black gloves. That painting has a dark area that abruptly truncates the man's right wrist. It looks unresolved. My guess is that his hand is disappearing inside a fold of the enormous red cushion that supports his back and head.

We now know Sargent retained this nude sketch in his personal collection. A few months after his death in 1925, his sisters consigned it to Christie's in London. It disappeared until 1999, when it surfaced at a Maine auction house.

I remember telling you that personal experiences had taught me not to assert anything regarding Sargent without "proof." It was a droll comment about the fact that my argument about his sexuality got a chilly reception from peers. You asserted a belief in artistic freedom and said poets are not constrained by that kind of burden of proof. Your spirited response made a big impression!

DP: I remain committed to seeing that shadow as a black glove. The title of the section in *Tender Voyeur* responding to that painting is "Male Venus Rising with One Black Leather Glove." It was important for me, and for my poem, to see a black glove when there probably wasn't any. Call it poetic license, if you will.

TF: What was your first poem connected in some way to Sargent's art? And when did you write it?

DP: My first piece about Sargent was this long poem in thirty-one sections, *Tender Voyeur*. I started it in 2005 and finished revising it in 2007, though I added three sections in 2021 and one in 2024. These additions are two sections to accommodate more biographical information that had come to light about Thomas E. McKeller, one of Sargent's main models at the end of his life; another section, a "found" poem from an index of first lines in *The Collected Poems of William Carlos Williams*; and the thirty-first section (2024), in which I wanted to show Nicola D'Inverno photographing Sargent, who had created so many images of Nicola.

TF: That means our original exchange happened early in your engagement with Sargent's work. I'm happy the glove poem belongs to that initial phase. Meanwhile, I've learned from our exchanges in 2022 that your interest in Sargent's art developed long before you addressed it through poetry.

DP: I saw some of his art at an early age because I grew up partly in Massachusetts, and because my parents were forever taking Michael, my brother with Down syndrome, and me to art museums. I was quite struck by two huge paintings in Boston: *El Jaleo* at the Gardner Museum and *The Daughters of Edward Darley Boit* at the MFA.

I also remember very distinctly *Fumée d'ambre gris* at the Clark Art Institute in Williamstown. It is a rather exoticized picture set in a Tangier courtyard. A woman in flowing white robes stands before a white column and white walls, perfuming herself over an open brazier of smoldering ambergris. Even as a kid, I knew that this scene was a manufactured fantasy of some sort. It is a study in white. There are only a few patches of color: the carpet, round cream floor tiles that have surrounding star points of blue, some red ribbons in the woman's attire, and her red nails and lips. Those details jump out at the viewer because of all that white.

And there's another painting at the Clark showing a man and woman talking in a shadowy alleyway in Venice. It is a long, narrow space with a glimpse of a sunlit piazza at its far end. I always felt the real hero of that painting is the wall on the left, where some of the plaster has fallen away and reveals lots of worn brickwork. Those bricks blur and look as if they're in motion. Sargent always responded with inspiration to textures, whether of fabric or, in this case, of a deteriorating wall. He made the wall as important as the figures or more so.

All of which is to say that I had some familiarity with Sargent before I eventually started to write *Tender Voyeur* at the tender age of forty-eight.

TF: Do you remember a eureka moment for *Tender Voyeur*?

DP: The moment of inspiration for the poem came from stumbling upon your book *John Singer Sargent: The Sensualist* sometime in 2005. I was smitten by those charcoal drawings of male nudes from Harvard's Fogg Museum, which you reproduced there and to which you had drawn attention in a much earlier essay. Your argument about the homoerotic side of Sargent's art made an immediate and galvanizing impression on me.

I now realize that you staked your professional career partly on your revolutionary revisionism in bringing the homoeroticism of Sargent's work to critical notice. How did you come to that viewpoint?

TF: After looking at hundreds of works by Sargent as a graduate student, I concluded that he took pleasure in depicting the male nude: the subject often inspired him to make particularly vivid images that were both sensual and technically superb. I assumed it was logical and pragmatic to ask if such a lifelong bachelor was attracted to his own sex. Mary Cassatt and Winslow Homer likewise never married, but to my eye, the bodies they depicted don't convey the emotion and physicality that I associate with Sargent when he was most enthralled by a model. My move was not popular, and I took the rap for "outing" him. But the topic was a bit of an open secret by 1980, and I heard peers make snide jokes. One curator referred to the showy brushwork in a painting of a rich woman as his "creampuff style," and another talked about the "faggy" watercolors at the Metropolitan Museum.

DP: When I started to send out homoerotic poems for publication around 2005 or so, I noticed how hard it was to get them published. Now, eighteen years later, literary journals seem much more willing to consider LGBTQ+ voices and include them. Has there been a similar change in the field of Sargent studies? Is there more genuine discussion about Sargent's sexuality among art historians and curators now?

TF: The tendency to dismiss the topic out of hand has abated, and a few people see the move as defensible and vital. Paul Fisher's 2022 biography presents itself as a game-changer on this score. It is a sign of the times when a major trade publisher gives a mainstream audience a work that, from beginning to end, tracks the issue of Sargent's sexuality. I don't know what impact it will have, but Fisher certainly focused on the artist as "an abiding enigma."

DP: I notice that in a footnote Fisher writes that you have "in a career of meticulous archival scholarship and careful art-historical analysis... made an increasingly compelling case for Sargent's presenting a complex 'repressed sexuality' and 'conflicted socio-sexual identity' as well as interpreting much of Sargent's work through dynamics of homoeroticism, disguise, and impersonation." Were there colleagues, mentors, or art historians who shared or encouraged your revisionist interpretation?"

TF: Richard Martin, a professor at the Fashion Institute of Technology, contacted me when he learned I was writing a dissertation on Sargent. He moonlighted as editor of *Arts Magazine*, and in that capacity welcomed two essays in 1981: the first was my unearthing of the "true story" of Madame X and the fallen shoulder strap that Sargent repainted after the portrait bombed at the Paris Salon; the second was about the homoerotic aura of an album of Sargent's charcoal drawings of nude male models.

Andy Warhol agreed to an interview in the galleries of the Sargent exhibition at the Whitney Museum in October, 1986, and *Arts Magazine* published it the following February, alongside an essay based on a Sargent lecture I'd recently given at the Whitney. Warhol's seemingly glib comments injected lots of gay innuendo, and he teased me about the fact that I ought to be able to confirm which of the handsome men Sargent drew and painted had been his "true friends." The Warhol interview meant little to the Americanist field at the time, but now I see it as a milestone in the narrative—his unabashed pleasure in tagging me, Sargent, and himself as fellow travelers.

The British art historian Richard Shone was incredibly generous when I was working on an essay for Norman Kleeblatt, curator at the Jewish Museum, New York. Richard directed me to a 1927 letter written by a member of London's unconventional, liberal coterie known as the Bloomsbury Group. It was an anecdotal report of a dinner party where people had discussed Sargent's sexuality: when the hostess, Ethel Sands, stated that he had "no sexual life at all," the French painter Jacques-Émile Blanche insisted he was a "frenzied bugger." (Both Sands and Blanche had known Sargent, and each was the subject of an oil portrait by him.) My essay, titled "The Complications of Being Sargent," made a splash when Norman debuted his 1999 exhibition of twelve of Sargent's oil paintings of the Wertheimer family.

I'm curious to know if you created any work involving same-sex attraction prior to the *Tender Voyeur* project?

DP: Yes, I started writing gay or homoerotic poems in 2003. I first became hyperconscious of my bisexuality through art. I was looking at reproductions of Michelangelo's sculptures and frescoes, particularly the four half-finished marble statues known as *Prisoners* or *Slaves*, when I first realized my sexual attraction. My first gay poem was entitled "Slave Awakening" after one of those statues. The name, as much as the image itself, was what seemed important to me since I saw myself, rather stereotypically, as 'awakening' to an 'enslaving' desire for men—terms that show me retrospectively as not feeling completely comfortable with my bisexual self. It was a shock at forty-six, in the middle of a long, monogamous, heterosexual marriage, to realize that I was bisexual. It took me some years to come to terms with that side of myself.

Obviously, *Tender Voyeur* was a way of recording that process of self-discovery and making it part of my conscious identity. And, of course, I came to realize that my bisexuality had existed long before then and been largely repressed from my teenage years through my early forties. A rather obscure online magazine called *Scythe* published "Slave Awakening" in 2009. I never included it in a collection because it didn't seem as strong as other gay poems written later.

TF: Michelangelo was the gateway, then Sargent became a muse. There's a wonderful reverberation there because Sargent tipped off the Metropolitan Museum about a superb Michelangelo chalk drawing that was coming on the market, and he helped broker the purchase in 1924. The work is a study for a female seer painted in fresco in the Sistine Ceiling, but the scholarly consensus today is that Michelangelo's model was a young male assistant.

DP: Ah, in the same way that Thomas McKeller served as the model for both male and female figures in the murals at Boston's Museum of Fine Arts. Do you think that both Michelangelo and Sargent, artists with great regard for the male body, depended so much on male models because they were sources of inspiration for them? Or was it simply a matter of it being easier for Michelangelo in his day to find a male model?

TF: I won't pronounce on Michelangelo, but I know that in Boston, starting in 1916, Sargent hired more than a dozen men and women to work as nude models. The African-American Thomas McKeller was certainly a favorite: he worked as a bellman at the hotel where Sargent and his valet lodged for two years (1916–18).

In 1994 I established that McKeller posed for at least three of the nude figures, one of them female, in Sargent's 1921 decoration *Classic and Romantic Art*, at the MFA. The artist paid him to model, but it is impossible to know whether McKeller enjoyed spending time with him, much less whether there was any personal warmth between the two men. Obviously, their interactions were governed by the settings in which they occurred: As an employee in the lobby of a fancy hotel, McKeller was subject to the societal and racist biases of American standards; but, in the protected privacy of Sargent's studio, he may have been free to express himself in a spirit of collaboration.

DP: Yes, there exists no historical record of the working relationship between McKeller and Sargent. Similarly, there are next-to-no documents about the twenty-five-year relationship between Sargent and his valet Nicola D'Inverno, whom he also painted and drew in charcoal and pencil numerous times. This absence of documentation, except for Sargent's images, offers me as a poet a tabula rasa on which to imagine Sargent's sexuality.

In the "fiction" of *Tender Voyeur*, which may or may not have any correspondence with reality, I imagine a long-standing sexual relationship between Sargent and his valet. *Tender Voyeur* further describes Sargent becoming attracted to McKeller so strongly that this desire is instrumental in severing his strong bond with Nicola. The artist and servant parted company in 1918. It is rumored that Nicola was involved in a bar brawl and Sargent dismissed him to avoid negative publicity. I posit Sargent's love for McKeller as the backstory that leads a frustrated Nicola to start that bar fight. *Tender Voyeur* respects what facts we have about Sargent's personal life but creates midrash around the very real gaps in that story.

While Sargent did not publicly exhibit his most homoerotic pictures, he displayed studies of handsome Italian models in his London residence. This closeting of homoerotic awareness echoed my own confusion about same-sex attraction for so many years. It was a great relief to me personally to be able to speak of my bisexuality openly. In Sargent and his images, I found a psychic correspondence. His sexuality was both "there" and "not there"—hiding in plain view—as was my own desire.

Then, in imagining a very specific sexual life for Sargent with D'Inverno, I was consciously exploring what homosexual life might have been like for Sargent and through him, for me. *Tender Voyeur* is an artistic act of self-projection.

TF: Your glove poem seems to present the reader with two acts of looking: You wonder what might have been on Sargent's mind when he was making the painting, and at the same time you are asking if your own responses to the picture tally with his reactions to the nude subject. Is that too simplistic?

DP: Maybe all of this interview is really both of us asking ourselves the questions that we are pretending to ask each other!

I think the glove poem, which is the final section of the original poem finished in 2007—and indeed the whole of *Tender Voyeur*—is driven by me trying to understand through Sargent's drawings and paintings myself as bisexual and to discover among his images a way of articulating that self and my desire. I recently attended a Zoom fiction reading by Robert Olen Butler. In a Q&A afterwards, he repeated the old adage that at the heart of all literary enterprise is the writer's urge to create a self or multiple selves. It reminds me of Whitman's poetic project in "Song of Myself," which I quote at the beginning of the glove section without naming the source. But, of course, my willful insertion of that black leather glove puts me and my more contemporary consciousness into play with the painting. Throughout the poem, I'm projecting my experience onto Sargent and hoping that he talks back. Kind of like the two of us here, going back and forth.

TF: People have projected assorted traits on Sargent's nude oil painting of Thomas McKeller. When I shepherded it into the permanent collection of the MFA in 1986, the biggest hurdle was full-frontal nudity. To convince the historically prim institution to purchase it, I stressed the backstory about the model: The Black Bostonian whose body was both "there" and "not there" in the Caucasian characters represented in the murals. It was a miracle that the MFA made the purchase. The picture readily appeals to artists and connoisseurs as a great example of Sargent's bravura style, but it also brings interpretative snags vis-à-vis the city's legacy of puritanism and racism.

In 2010 the MFA's gay director, Malcolm Rogers, orchestrated its spectacular apotheosis by hanging it in the large gallery devoted to Sargent in the new Art of the Americas Wing. Rogers's installation on brocade-covered walls, and the way he favored Sargent over Homer and Eakins, was a cheeky challenge to former hierarchies. But the novelty wore off quickly. In 2020 the Isabella Stewart Gardner Museum made waves in the national press with *Boston's Apollo*, an exhibition that spotlighted the Black model as an "unsung hero" and portrayed his collaboration with Sargent as a chapter "erased" by historians. During polarized times, the project symbolized the museum's move to be a supporter of Black Lives Matter and an ally to LGBTQ+ people. It asked if and how racism and same-sex attraction affected the relationship between artist and model.

DP: I didn't see the exhibition, which occurred during the pandemic, but purchased the catalog immediately and read it from cover to cover. In fact, the catalog presented material about McKeller that was new to me and inspired two additional sections of *Tender Voyeur*. I noticed, of course, that you were a contributor...

TF: Yes, the tenor of catalog was unusual for the Sargent field. I didn't see the show because my relationship with the project was awkward. In February 2017, I met with the Gardner's Director and the Curator of the Collection and offered to curate a Sargent exhibition. One idea for a show that I mentioned over lunch was the male nude, which could include the drawings of McKeller he gave to Mrs. Gardner. I eventually suggested a show about Sargent, Gardner, and Symbolism in Boston, and in March the Director politely declined my offer. In April I was invited back by the Curator and Associate Curator (Nathaniel Silver) to look at the nude drawings and left that meeting with the impression that Silver and I would plan a show together. Then Silver went radio silent until July 2018, when he told me he was organizing a Sargent/McKeller exhibition and expressed hope that I would contribute to his catalog. Given my scholarship on Sargent and Boston, it would have been foolish not to participate, so I wrote about the context in which the MFA made its landmark 1986 acquisition of *Nude Study of Thomas E. McKeller*. Silver's show opened in February 2020, and the Gardner successfully pitched the McKeller story to critics and reporters as its discovery.

DP: *Boston's Apollo* has inspired composer Damien Geter and librettist Lila Palmer to compose a new opera. *American Apollo* portrays a fictionalized sexual relationship between McKeller and Sargent. The Des Moines Metro Opera commissioned this work and presented it in the summer of 2024 to enthusiastic reviews by the *New Yorker*, *Wall Street Journal*, and *Opera Today*. Though I was unable to attend any of the performances, the opera's last scene apparently features McKeller viewing Sargent's nude portrait of him for the first time after the painter's death. Would you comment on this latest development in the changing reception of Sargent, specifically his relationship with his inspiring Black model?

TF: I did not see the opera, but I read the synopsis of the libretto. It sounds as though the creators imaginatively extrapolated the Sargent/McKeller scenario to the familiar paradigms of opera—a budding romance; circumstances and foes that unleash emotional suffering; the fate of dreams and longings. It could be that this is an ideal medium in which to consider the emotional and sensual aspects of Sargent's life, which are easily glimpsed in the way he painted and essentially inscrutable in his public persona. The opera could broach Sargent's private life for a wide public audience: Seeing ideas and feelings unfold on stage could win over far more people than four decades of hairsplitting scholarly skirmishes!

Saying that makes me reflect on my feelings about being involved in the progress of your poetry project *Tender Voyeur*. First, I felt maneuvered by *Boston's Apollo*, then I had no connections to *American Apollo*, but now I have been recognized and welcomed as your book developed. When I look at its table of contents, I see that the original twenty-seven-section work, augmented by its four new sections, is now framed with two later poems that are more obliquely about Sargent. I think there are parallels between my Sargenting and your *Tender Voyeur*, because each of us was traveling on a rocky road.

DP: Yes, I made the conscious choice not to try to publish *Tender Voyeur* after finishing revisions on it in 2007. My wife was not comfortable with the fact that I was starting to write and slowly publish homosexual verse. She refused to read any poem of mine that spoke of homoerotic desire. Understandably, she felt threatened and upset. I believed that our marriage would not have been able to withstand the strain if *Tender Voyeur* were to have been published. Eventually, in 2019, we separated and got divorced a year later. I decided that it would be aesthetically compelling to book-end the text of the 2007 *Tender Voyeur* with two later poems focusing on the dissolution of the marriage since some of the seeds of that dissolution were contained in *Tender Voyeur*. Unfortunately, I felt that my bisexuality could never be freely and openly acknowledged within my marriage.

In a larger context, let me say that male bisexuality is all too often not accepted or acknowledged by either the heteronormative population or by the male gay community. The latter sometimes dismisses bisexuality as a "phase" that a man passes through to discover his true homosexuality. The straight world also tends to question its existence. For instance, in 2005, the *New York Times* reported positively on a study by Professor Michael Baily of Northwestern University, who claimed to find no scientific basis for male bisexuality. Six years later, Baily acknowledged flaws in his original findings and concluded that male bisexuals do exist. The *Times* eventually recanted in 2014, with a cover story in its magazine announcing the "rediscovery" of male bisexuality.

I think this gender position is disquieting to so many individuals because it eludes categorization and is, therefore, perceived as dangerous, disjunctive, and insidious. Certainly, during the AIDS crisis, male bisexuals were blamed for spreading AIDS to the heterosexual population. Because of these sorts of cultural stigma, male bisexuals are often hesitant to come out.

While there exists a long and rich tradition of gay male poetry in English, particularly from Whitman onwards, there does not seem to me to be a corresponding tradition of male bisexual poetry that acknowledges and celebrates the delights and tensions of dual attraction. A poetics of bisexual desire is explored by Catullus, one of whose poems I translate in *Tender Voyeur*, by Shakespeare in his sonnets, by Lord Byron, and perhaps by Melville with his depiction of Ishmael and Queequeg's relationship in *Moby-Dick*, which I perversely count as a kind of epic poem. Despite these stellar exemplars of bisexual subjectivity among poets, a Google search for "male bisexual poets" tends to yield many modern and contemporary writers who identify primarily, or exclusively, as "gay." When one looks at the recent Lambda Literary Awards in Bisexual Poetry, it's striking that books by bisexual women predominate. If the *Times Literary Supplement* were to run want ads, I might submit: "Male bisexual poet seeks to enter into literary correspondence with others of his species, *O rara avis!*"

That rare bird might take us back to the painting of Thomas McKeller by Sargent. I've always loved the wings that surround the model's shoulders. They are related to an MFA mural roundel of Prometheus chained to a rock and having his liver eaten by a vulture, wings spread, for stealing fire from the gods and giving it to humankind. Can you comment on the happy artistic decision not to go mythological, but instead to paint the naked man's beauty and yet keep those wings behind him?

TF: What you describe began as an ordinary studio decision. I suspect Sargent made the nude portrait on impulse, and he used a canvas that was readily at hand—one that happened to have a rudimentary image of his Prometheus design. He probably completed the nude portrayal of McKeller in one sitting. Had he intended to exhibit it in public, he would have eliminated all traces of the earlier Prometheus study and made the background consistently shadowy.

I hope that the artist decided to stop painting when he did because he registered the unfinished background had a poetic or abstract dimension. Even if that's not the case, a century later many viewers do enjoy that accidental juxtaposition of a radiant muscular physique and a setting that suggests spectral wings.

As you suggest, the image of McKeller is utterly non-mythological because it observes physical reality so sincerely. There's a chasm between it and the MFA murals. When Sargent adapted that physique for the bodies of gods and goddesses, the finished products were idealized and decorous. The magic of the nude portrait sketch is that it exalts the fleshly realm of studio work. I think Sargent was paying tribute to a man he cherished. In that painting McKeller looks simultaneously earthy, humane, and resolute. I hope it was the artist's intention to make a painting of a man he considered beautiful on those three counts.

A Letter

Written by Trevor Fairbrother to Donald Platt

Dear Don,

I love the way *Tender Voyeur* coaxes readers to think about being in a room with Sargent. What's happening? This happened? You don't mince words regarding the erotic and the corporeal. You are a poet, and you communicate emotions. You write: "His long cock rests / on his white right thigh." The sentence begins in the middle of one line and ends on the next. Art historians and curators who write about Sargent don't say "cock." They mostly want to enshrine a cosmopolitan society portraitist: someone who produced vivid "speaking likenesses" that magically take on an Old Master-ish aura of distinction.

Newcomers to Sargent studies have to grapple with the man's volatile reputation. There's a century of capricious ratings from commentators who had to come to terms with the fact he was too clever and successful for his own good. As early as 1910, some were tiring of the way the mainstream press idolized him. Shifts in taste were inevitable for a new generation, but envy was a consideration with such detractors as Walter Sickert, Jacques-Émile Blanche, and Roger Fry, who were both artists and writers. Soon after Sargent's death, modernist crusaders gutted his prestige. In addition, partisan Americans characterized his stance as Eurocentric and self-serving. Lewis Mumford branded him an illustrator rather than an artist in *Brown Decades* (1931). The text warned that bravura brushwork and a "dashing eye for effect" ultimately failed to hide "the essential emptiness of Sargent's mind." A revival of interest in his work began modestly in the 1950s. By 2000 a run of blockbuster exhibitions had turned his showiest pictures into multimillion-dollar acquisitions for trophy hunters. That adulation continues, and contemporary cheerleaders prefer not to mention the very real backlash to Sargent that accompanied the Depression and the ascendancy of modernist abstraction.

These historic disputes haunt the topic of the artist's sexuality. Parallel biases in the marketplace probably made the "confirmed bachelor" situation more tortuous. Anything with a whiff of homoeroticism or Wildean decadence was swept under the carpet. Marsden Hartley's same-sex interests were an open secret by the 1930s, but curators and dealers glossed over the evidence until the late twentieth century. No wonder, then, that the situation with Sargent—born a generation before Hartley—was more deeply repressed. His career was soaring in 1895 when Oscar Wilde was incarcerated for "gross indecency." The painter and writer met in Paris in the early 1880s. When the smart set exalted them, each maintained a residence on Tite Street. Sargent surely feared the likelihood of professional disaster should his male nudes foster rumor.

What follows are statements from published texts. Each in its way sheds light on the contentious climate of opinion regarding sexuality. Collectively, they are a measure of the disregard and suppression favored by gatekeepers.

1925

"He never married. He was a secluded and inscrutable personality.... Whether the revelation of unpleasant traits seen in some of his [portrait] paintings has been satire or pure realism is a question on which the artist never had anything to say." This appeared in the *New York Times* ("J. S. Sargent Dies in Sleep in London," April 16). Even if Sargent himself maintained strict privacy, the words hinted that he was gifted with powers to probe and reveal.

1926

"Two things stand out in my memory of him—his unfailing benevolence where the welfare of art was concerned, and his inscrutability in all that touched his purely personal life. He was strong in all things; always giving sympathy, never evoking it, always helpful to others, and always self-contained—a strange mixture of a compassionate Christian and a stoical Red Indian Warrior!" Percy Grainger made this comment in a tribute written for inclusion in the Sargent biography by Evan Charteris. Grainger was a piano prodigy and composer of experimental "free music." He and Sargent bonded over music. While discreet about his sexual preferences (masochism with female partners), he was open about them to friends. Sargent befriended both Charteris and Grainger (who sat for a portrait in charcoal in 1908).

1955

"[Sargent] was a large and strong man, with, if one knew him at all, enough indications of virility not to be taken for an example of the intellectualized homosexuality notable among artists in London.... The young musicians who trailed him everywhere were thought effeminate. He had some strange friends, some of whom appeared to have relationships among themselves of which society, though aware of in an oblique way, did not openly approve.... Yet it was impossible to believe that [he] could be anything but the vigorously masculine individual he seemed." Charles Merrill Mount wrote this in *John Singer Sargent: A Biography*. Mount was born in Brooklyn as Sherman Merrill Suchow and trained as a painter in New York. His book on Sargent was the first of three biographies. He was later accused of painting and selling fake Sargents, and in 1987 went to prison for stealing historic documents from national institutions.

1965

"Reserved and austere, with his imposing bulk and bulging eyes, he was only at ease with his family and close friends, detesting social occasions and the flattery of the fashionable world. His life was dedicated to his art, and his apparently mysterious private life held no secrets beyond his easel and his paint brush." Richard Ormond wrote this in "The Case of John Singer Sargent" (*The Saturday Book*, 25th annual issue). Two of the illustrations showed superb works owned by his father, Conrad Ormond, who was Sargent's nephew: *Mosquito Nets* (1908) and *Nude Man on Bed* (1917). Ormond had included both in the 1964 Sargent exhibition he curated at the Birmingham Museum and Art Gallery, England. As the grandson of Sargent's sister, Violet, his caginess about Sargent's private life may have reflected familial bonds and expectations. (In 2014 he wrote, "I grew up surrounded by Sargent's work in the houses of my parents, my uncles and aunt, and my grandmother.")

1986

"[The long association between Sargent and his manservant] has often been incorrectly treated to the high gloss of homosexual love.... Sargent housed no secrets in his soul, which was maddeningly never opened for scrutiny. He was not designed for the usual varieties of intimacy: his single brief experiment with [Miss] Louise Burckhardt [in Paris in 1881] revealed only an ability to try and no fluency.... No one who knew him well or slightly has ever been tempted to suggest anything whatever about his private life." Stanley Olson, born in Akron, Ohio, made these assertions in *John Singer Sargent: His Portrait*. In the early 1970s he had the means and panache to transform himself into an English *bon vivant*, mustering surviving members of the Bloomsbury Group while writing a thesis on Virginia and Leonard Woolf's Hogarth Press.

1987

In February the following article appeared in *Arts Magazine*: Trevor J. Fairbrother, "Warhol Meets Sargent at Whitney." It was based on my interview with Andy Warhol in the galleries of the Whitney Museum's Sargent retrospective. As a member of the American art department at the MFA Boston, I insinuated that my curatorial peers lived in denial about Sargent's bachelor status, and the insouciant Pop artist picked up on my camp understatement. In this excerpt, we are looking at a charcoal portrait of Mrs. Charles Hunter:

AW: Is this Mrs. Sargent?

TF: No.

AW: Was there a Mrs. Sargent?

TF: No. He didn't marry—like Henry James.

AW: There wasn't a Mrs. James?

TF: No. Are you surprised?

AW: Yeah, I'm surprised. Well, tell me all the stuff—you mean there's a big story to his life?

TF: No, we don't know.

AW: You don't know? You know everything.

TF: The scholars don't know. What do you think?

AW: Well I don't know.

TF: Can you tell?

AW: You mean nobody talks about him?

TF: I guess not.

AW: Really? Not one person? There must be a story, you just don't want to tell it to us.

TF: Scholars aren't supposed to…

AW: dwell…?

1998

"[Sargent] did not relish intimacy, and he avoided emotional entanglements likely to complicate his life and compromise his independence. If he had sexual relationships, they must have been of a brief and transient nature, and they have left no trace. The answer is that we simply do not know, and decoding messages from his work is no substitute for evidence." Richard Ormond made this declaration in the essay he contributed to the notable exhibition catalogue *John Singer Sargent*; he and Elaine Kilmurray co-curated the project for the Tate Gallery, London. Both exhibition and catalog had thematic sections devoted to the murals, but excluded *Nude Study of Thomas E. McKeller*. When the show traveled to Boston in 1999, the Museum of Fine Arts tucked its painting into the display.

2000

"Some people feel that there's simply not enough evidence...to talk seriously about [Sargent's possible homosexuality]. There are drawings that have a distinct homoerotic character. Does it affect his art? I don't think [it is] the key to Sargent's art that unlocks dimensions of it that we haven't seen before." The PBS TV documentary *John Singer Sargent: Outside the Frame* included this opinion in its excerpts from an interview with Nicolai Cikovsky Jr., curator at the National Gallery, Washington.

2001

"The Seattle show is especially interesting because it shows two very different sides of Sargent's work. On one hand you have the Wertheimer portraits, which are formal pictures made to be installed in a very elegant and important home. Then you have this large group of nude male studies, which are totally personal. You see the bipolar aspect of Sargent. He's an incredible public artist who does grandiose commissions, but also a very private person engaged in his own artistic investigations, which I'm convinced are partly about some sort of sexual longing." Norman Kleebatt, the curator for fine arts at the Jewish Museum, made this comment about *John Singer Sargent: The Sensualist*, the exhibition I curated for the Seattle Art Museum in 2000. He was quoted in Stephen Kinzer's review in the *New York Times*, March 15, 2001.

2001

"When I talk to people, gay and straight, I don't find widespread agreement about the eroticism of [Sargent's charcoal drawings of male nudes]. Some see them as just facile exaggerations of studio-nude conventions. Heterosexual men have told me they look like locker-room nudes—the kind of athletic male bodies they admire in sporting events. They see an identification with these bodies on the artist's part, but not necessarily sexual intimacy." Martha Kingsbury, a professor of art history, made this remark to Patricia Failing, who presented it in her essay "The Hidden Sargent" (*Artnews*, May, 2001).

2001

"[I congratulate Fairbrother for] changing the terms of Sargent scholarship [and] forcing people to deal with the implications of sexuality. [His Seattle show] is courageous, growing out of years of work that was resisted. [The artist's mainstream sensuousness has always been recognized,] but now there's the possibility of another kind of sensuousness, which relates to the forbidden. Sargent's work seems to be appealing to a wide range of possible desires and suggests the need for a complex, fluid view of human sexuality. Masquerade has become an issue for Sargent studies, making him a much more relevant artist in contemporary terms. [The exhibition] should make us all reconsider why Sargent's painting, which used to seem so empty, has cast such a spell over audiences at the end of this century." Jonathan Weinberg, an artist, art historian and critic, quoted by Patricia Failing, in "The Hidden Sargent" (*Artnews*, May, 2001).

2003

"Going by the paintings in the exhibition, it seems Sargent's interest in women was, by turns, filial, fraternal and Platonic but never sexual. [In his work] you never sense the kind of carnal desire that you do in artists like Ingres, Renoir, Gérôme and others who made women a major subject.... Curiously, considering the theme of the show, the catalog essayists conspicuously avoid the question of Sargent's sexual orientation. For the Sargent scholar Richard Ormond, this artist's 'emotional reticence and fear of intimacy' may have had something to do with his mother, Mary Newbold Sargent. She was evidently quite a piece of work: 'flighty, impulsive, dramatic, emotional, self-centered, domineering, sociable, temperamental, manipulative and always in delicate health.' Mr. Ormond speculates that Sargent's total immersion in art was in part an escape from her influence." Ken Johnson, an art critic for the *New York Times*, aired those thoughts in his review of *Sargent's Women*, an exhibition at Adelson Galleries (December 5). I think he was amused to find psychobiography invoked in an obvious effort to designate the female subject as the artist's prime attraction. Johnson challenged the project's heterosexist procedure by concluding that Sargent's depictions of women were low on "lascivious desire" and rich in "romantic identification" with individuals in whom he sensed "independence of mind and spirit."

2010

Writing in *Houston's Sargents*, the book published by the Museum of Fine Arts, Houston, in conjunction with an exhibition of that name, Richard Ormond altered his stance on the artist's private life: "Though his art was anything but sexless, Sargent never married, there were no intimate relationships we know about and he was possibly homosexual by inclination."

OK, Don, imagine a reader who wants to learn more about two paintings of naked male models that guided your words in *Tender Voyeur*. In the earlier, slightly smaller work a seated white man leans back into a red cushion and directs his gaze at the viewer (p. 135); in the other, a Black man kneels on a rectangular stand, his buttocks supported by a green cushion, with his raised head looking upward (p. 121). The convenient way to begin such an exploration is to consult the nine-volume catalogue raisonné co-authored by Elaine Kilmurray and Richard Ormond: *John Singer Sargent: The Complete Paintings*, published between 1998 and 2016.

The first painting can be found in the chapter "Models and Life Studies, 1901–1907" (Vol. VII, 2012). Kilmurray and Ormond resurrected the title used by Christie's in 1925 when the firm auctioned items from Sargent's estate: *A Male Model, Seated; Red Cushion Background*. The sixteen works in this chapter depict a motley crew of dark-haired males—fifteen men and one boy. The authors decided that it was not possible to identify any of them by name. Even though others had previously touted the first five pictures in their line-up as depictions of D'Inverno, Sargent's manservant, they decided there was insufficient information to warrant those claims. Their entry on the painting with the red cushion was a brief banal description ("The model is uncomfortably posed...").

The second work can be found in the chapter "Mural-Related and Classical Studies, c. 1891–1920" (Vol. IX, 2016). It received the title *Nude Study of Thomas E. McKeller* when the Museum of Fine Arts, Boston, purchased it in 1986. I worked in the Department of American Paintings at the time and shepherded it into the collection. I argued the importance of recognizing that the body of Sargent's favorite local model—an African American—inspired numerous idealized light-skinned characters in his neoclassical murals at the MFA. In my 1994 Sargent monograph I proved that McKeller's body was the basis of female as well as male figures pictured in those decorations. The 2016 catalogue entry by Kilmurray and Ormond was erroneous about the model's place of birth and the picture's exhibition history, and, perversely, it used "McKellar" for his surname, favoring the misspelling introduced in print in 1956 by David McKibbin (the librarian at the Boston Athenaeum who had laid the groundwork for their catalogue raisonné).

The artist kept the two male nudes under discussion in his personal collection and never published or exhibited them. Those decisions were doubtless conditioned by the subject matter and the air of sensuality. Stories behind these paintings afford a few glimpses of Sargent's working life. I think it likely that the model in the first work was D'Inverno (1873–1931), an Italian who grew up in a large immigrant family in London. He first modeled for Sargent in 1892 and soon became his full-time aide. He married Emily Askey in December 1897. By 1901 the couple had moved into Sargent's recently enlarged premises in Chelsea, working as valet and cook. They had no children.

In 1916 Sargent and D'Inverno traveled to Boston, anticipating a lengthy stay that would be focused on the long-overdue mural decorations at the Boston Public Library. Comfortably lodged at the Hotel Vendome for two years, the two Londoners befriended the man depicted in the second nude painting, Thomas McKeller (1890–1962), an unmarried bellman at the hotel. McKeller grew up in Wilmington, North Carolina, and moved to Boston in his early twenties. He probably began modeling for Sargent in 1916.

As Sargent prepared to return to England in 1918, D'Inverno left his employ and sought American citizenship. Before embarking, Sargent wrote a will and included a modest bequest to his valet: the sum was enough for a comfortable trip back to London. As it happened, D'Inverno abandoned his wife and made his living in Boston as a factory worker and a cleaner. By 1930 he was a janitor in New York City, where he died the following year. Meanwhile, McKeller ceased work as a bellman in 1918 and joined a US regiment. He did not see combat and resumed work as a Boston model in 1919. He became a Post Office employee in 1924, and he married Rena Meads a decade later.

Maintaining that there is no "secure comparative image" of D'Inverno, the authors of *Complete Paintings* hedged about works that might represent him. This was surprising because the mustachioed Italian included a head shot of himself in his memoir about Sargent, published in the *Boston Sunday Advertiser* early in 1926. I relied on that photo in 1981 when proposing that one charcoal drawing in a bound compilation of male nude

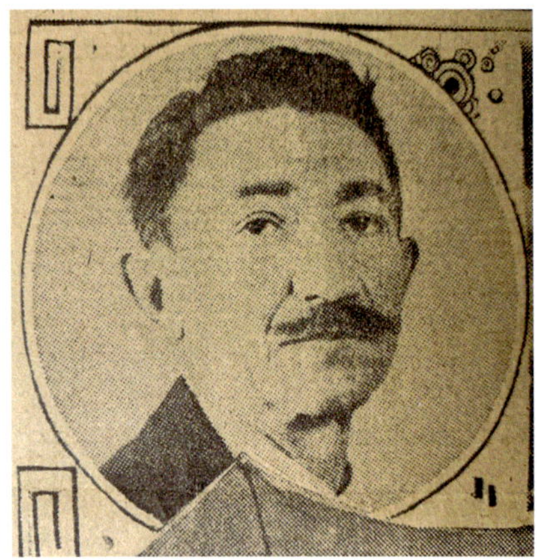

"The REAL John Singer Sargent, as His Valet Saw Him," *Boston Sunday Advertiser*, February 7, 1926. In the caption D'Inverno stated that he was "for nearly a quarter of a century model, valet and house-manager of the late John Singer Sargent." He also illustrated two of his photographs of Sargent: one making a watercolor in the Alps, the other on horseback in Montana.

studies portrayed D'Inverno (p. 85). That work was a comparative illustration in *Complete Paintings* (Vol. VII, as cited above), but Kilmurray and Ormond made no comment on it. On the other hand, they stated D'Inverno was "almost certainly" the model for a few outdoor pictures and identified him in *The Chess Game* (1907) and *Mountain Stream* (1914). The latter is a watercolor that shows a naked bather in the middle distance with his back to the viewer.

Even if the subject of *A Male Model, Seated* (p. 135) is not D'Inverno, he typifies the Mediterranean men whose bodies inspired Sargent's picture-making throughout four decades. All such works might be sidelined as "studies"—exercises that any painter trained in the Beaux-Arts tradition might undertake—but we know that Sargent prized and exhibited several examples. In 1903, when he oversaw *The Work of John S. Sargent, R.A.*, a survey of his own accomplishments, he included several pictures of this sort. The hefty and expensive volume featured a sequence of paintings of striking non-Anglo men and women: *Bedouin Arab*; *Egyptian Girl* (p. 91); *Italian with Rope*; and *Egyptian Woman (Coin Necklace)*. The first and third were bust-length images of handsome men, the second a full-length female nude, and the last a head in profile; none of the subjects was identified by name.

Sargent's erotic identity continues to inspire baffling incidents. In 2017 several cultural institutions in the UK commemorated the fiftieth anniversary of the partial decriminalization of sex between men in England and Wales in 1967. The end products included two landmark publications that illustrated portraits by Sargent: *Queer British Art: 1861–1967* (the catalogue of an exhibition at Tate Britain, London) and *Prejudice & Pride: Celebrating LGBTQ Heritage* (a souvenir booklet published by the British National Trust to cap its ambitious yearlong public programming). The good news was that each effort brought insightful information about people portrayed by Sargent, and the bad news was the artist's sexual identity went unmentioned. The subjects of these portraits were honored as singular examples of eccentric sexuality, but there was no recognition that Sargent's own transgressive experiences and perspective probably bolstered the aesthetic success of the works in question.

The Sargent in the Tate's exhibition was the 1881 portrait sketch of his friend Violet Page, whose nom de plume, Vernon Lee, could suggest a man or a woman. Violet/Vernon established deeply felt relationships with women, and never married. In a bravura performance Sargent evoked a lively intellectual presence with glasses and plain, smart attire. The National Trust's publication included the 1923 charcoal bust of Robert Gould Shaw III, a dashing, fair-haired twenty-something wearing the dark blue frockcoat of the Household Cavalry. In his day, he had a criminal record that flagged him as a "homosexual"—in 1931, he was sentenced to six months in prison for solicitation. Prior to his arrest, Shaw hid his sexuality from his mother and stepfather, the Viscount Astor. The social censure he faced prompted his stepbrother, David Astor, to support the reform campaign that eventually led to the breakthrough 1967 Sexual Offenses Act.

In 2022 Paul Fisher, a professor of American Studies, attempted to evoke "a more unpredictable and border-crossing" version of the artist in his book *The Grand Affair: John Singer Sargent in His World* (2022). He culled myriad observations from the recent Sargent literature and postulated correspondences with charged issues trending in the 2020s: same-sex interests, gender nonconformity, ethnicity, race, and global commerce. Fisher foregrounded the possibility of the artist's "sexual nonconformity" while declining to describe him as "homosexual" or "gay"—because such labeling would allow academics and queer theorists to dismiss his argument as ahistorical. Writing about this biography in *The Gay and Lesbian Review*, Andrew Holleran astutely diagnosed the inconclusive scenario. He warned readers that the text adopted the "academically honorable route of saying that all the evidence is ambiguous—a circumspection that becomes frustrating after a while, however justified." Holleran, a pioneer of post-Stonewall gay literature, explained that Fisher had no "paper trail" at his disposal, which forced him to focus on Sargent's friendships and affinities that might serve as grist for discourse in the new age of Queer Studies: "It's as if the whole book is written in gaydar. There is no evidence, but much guilt by association."

A recent international Sargent exhibition (Boston and London, 2023–24) examined his portraits through the lens of dress and fashion. It was the first "blockbuster" to allow that the artist's engagement with gender and sexuality were not without complexity and subversion. One of the curators, Caroline Corbeau-Parsons, made a formal nod by referring to "the much debated and unresolved question of Sargent's (homo)sexuality." The English journalist Hermione Eyre followed suit with this remark: "Sargent was, possibly, curious about, but ultimately left cold by, the mysteries of heterosexual love. He destroyed a great part of his own letters and papers, but he left sketchbooks of male nudes full of intimacy and expertise" (*Daily Telegraph*, February 10, 2024). Only Charlie Porter, an openly gay fashion journalist and historian, had the nerve to imply that the analysis was cursory: "[Writing about the artist usually demurs] from discussing the implications of his sexuality. There is still prudishness when talking about queerness and Sargent, who left no letters or diaries that give facts about his lovers.... To understand the role of fashion in his public works, I believe that we should also consider the implications of clothing in the art he kept hidden. They might even give us insight into the complexity and repressions of the gay male experience around a century ago.... [If] we stick with a traditional reading [of the artist's interest in fashion], I believe that we keep Sargent, ourselves, fashion, and art, caught in the trap" (*Financial Times*, February 16, 2024).

Let me end by saying again that there is nothing comparable to your new book in the Sargent literature. You conjure Sargent as an intensely visual person who never tired of looking. *Tender Voyeur* is an honest and glowing curveball rooted in the time you have spent loving people and pictures. I think we agree that discussions of the artist's sexuality have been both encouraging and frustrating: It is exciting to see explorations of his so-called queer milieu, but dispiriting when writers refuse to say that it is extremely likely and probable that Sargent was a "love that dare not speak its name" closet case. What *Tender Voyeur* does, starting as early as 2005, is to take the artistic and logical step into the realm of "what if" analysis. What might the same-sex relationships in Sargent's life have looked like?

Thank you,

Trevor.

Note: I dedicate this essay to Robert Pickavance, a longtime friend who gleaned significant information about the life and family of Nicola D'Inverno. Three amazing archivists—Shana McKenna, Maureen Melton, and Carolle Morini—could not have been kinder. I also give thanks to David Deiss, John T. Kirk, and Christopher J. Warren. Finally, I want to express my deepest appreciation to Donald Platt, Elizabeth Murphy, and Grid Books for this opportunity to reflect freely on my experiences as a Sargent scholar.

Notes

Tender Voyeur describes a long-standing love affair between the artist John Singer Sargent and his manservant Nicola D'Inverno. Though there is no documented basis for such an intimate relationship, it exists as an historical possibility, one which the speaker of this poem explores fictionally for his own purposes. Trevor Fairbrother, curator, art historian, and critic, has persuasively delineated the homoerotic nature of many of Sargent's images in his book *John Singer Sargent: The Sensualist* (Yale, 2000). My poem, the original draft of which was written between 2005 and 2007, draws liberally on the wealth of detail that Fairbrother has assembled therein and derives much of its inspiration from his work. Many later critics, including Christopher Capozolla, Dorothy Moss, Alan Chong, the fiction writer Colm Tóibín, and the biographer Paul Fisher, have built upon, and explored, Fairbrother's interpretation of Sargent's oeuvre as informed by homosexual desire. Indeed, Fisher's biography *The Grand Affair* (Farrar, Straus & Giroux, 2022) retraces much of the material originally advanced by Fairbrother and concludes not only that Sargent lived largely in, and was part of, the "queer" culture of his day, but that, contextually, an intimate relationship between Nicola D'Inverno and Sargent was highly probable.

While any love affair between Sargent and D'Inverno may remain hypothetical, most of the surrounding details, quotations, and biographical data in *Tender Yoyeur* are not.

However, I want to acknowledge one lapse in my research. In the summer of 2023, long after the original draft of my poem was complete, I learned from Trevor Fairbrother's letter to me (published at the end of this book) that D'Inverno got married in 1897, perhaps four years or so after he started working for Sargent. By 1901, he and his wife, Emily Askey, had moved into Sargent's Tite Street residence. Nicola continued to work as Sargent's valet and Emily as cook. I also learned that Emily did not accompany Sargent and D'Inverno to Boston in 1916. After Sargent and D'Inverno separated in 1918, Nicola never returned to London, or Emily, but remained in the US and died in New York City in 1931. Emily and Nicola had no children. I would have liked to write some sections around these new-to-me facts but found that the structure of the original poem made it difficult. Mostly, though, it was hard for me to reenter the poem and draft new material in that older style. Therefore, *Tender Voyeur* will always remain somewhat flawed in that it omits known facts in this one important instance.

Below is a bibliography of the works that I've used to research *Tender Voyeur* and brief notes about the quotations in the poem's thirty-one sections.

D'Inverno, Nicola. "The REAL John Singer Sargent, as His Valet Saw Him." Boston: *Boston Sunday Advertiser*, February 7, 1926. (*RS*)

Davis, Helga and Belcham, Derrick. *Boston's Apollo: Sargent and McKeller* (YouTube video). Produced by the Isabella Stewart Gardner Museum, 2020: https://www.youtube.com/watch?v=TnmdEARSSwE (*BASM)*

Ellman, Richard. *Oscar Wilde*. New York: Knopf, 1988. (*OW*)

Fairbrother, Trevor. *John Singer Sargent: The Sensualist.* New Haven and London: Yale University Press, 2000. (*SS*)

Hoopes, Donelson, Walsh, Judith, and Strickler, Susan E. *American Traditions in Watercolor: The Worcester Art Museum Collection*. New York: Abbeville Press, 1987. (*ATW*)

Ratcliff, Carter. *John Singer Sargent.* New York: Artabras Publishers, 1982. (*JS*)

Silver, Nathaniel, editor. *Boston's Apollo*. Boston: Isabella Stuart Gardner Museum Publications, 2020. (*BA*)

Troyen, Carol. *Sargent's Murals in the Museum of Fine Arts, Boston.* Boston: Museum of Fine Arts, 1999. (*SM*)

IV. Betty Wertheimer's quote, *SS*, 220.

V. The quote from the "sitter," Jacques-Émile Blanche who was a contemporary painter, is recorded in *SS*, 220. The exchange between Sargent and Robertson, *JS*, 240.

VI. Sargent's quote, *SS*, 18.

VIII. Sargent's letter, *JS*, 219. The guide's name, Hastings, has been invented since no document lists it.

IX. D'Inverno's quotes, *RS*.

X. D'Inverno's quote about the portrait of Woodrow Wilson, *RS*

XI. D'Inverno's quotes, *RS*.

XIII. Sargent's response to his critics, *SS*, 18. Sargent's letter to Vernon Lee, *JS*, 80. His friend Ralph Curtis's quote is paraphrased from *JS*, 84. The line by Blake is from "The Proverbs of Heaven and Hell."

XVI. D'Inverno's quote, *RS*.

XVII. The passage from Catullus's poem 56 is translated by the author.

XVIII. The translation of Catullus's poem 48 is the author's.

XIX. The three biblical quotes are respectively from II Samuel, 1:26; I Samuel, 18: 4; I Samuel, 20: 30. Wilde's quote while on trial, *OW*, 463. Wilde's letter to Bosie, *OW,* 461. Wilde's letter to Ross, *OW,* 385. The Marquess of Queensbury's quote, *OW,* 418. Bosie's telegram to his father, *OW,* 418. Inscription on the Marquess of Queensbury's calling card, *OW,* 438. Wilde's quote in French about Bosie ("The prince of caprice has departed for Capri."), *OW,* 482. Exchange between Wilde and Reggie Turner, *OW,* 581. Quoted description of Wilde's bodily explosion at death, *OW,* 584.

XX. Thomas Fox's quote, *SS,* 176. Quote from the "art critic," *SM,* 14.

XXI. Sargent's quote, *BA*, 211. McKeller's quote, *BA*, 231. Deidre McKeller O'Bryant's quote, *BASM*, 7:09–7:30.

XXIV. D'Inverno's three quotes ("money fever"; "He would not pay..."; and "The only priceless..."), *RS.* The quote beginning "as an official war artist...," is a composite of statements from *JS,* 197–201. Sargent's quote about "fighting on the Sabbath" is a slightly modified version of the original statement, *JS,* 201. The quotation from the Criminal Law Amendment Act, *OW*, 409. Queen Victoria's quote, *OW*, 409. The last line of this section ("the mesmeric swing of that kilt") is a quotation from a letter by Neil Bartlett to Trevor Fairbrother in 1999, *SS,* 222.

XXVII. The italicized lines from various flamenco songs are English translations taken from Nimbus Records' *Cante Gitano*, 1989. The singers who improvised these lines are José de la Tomasa, María la Burra, and María Soléa.

XXX. The quotation from Thoreau is from *Walden*, the chapter "Where I Lived, and What I Lived For." The sitter quoted is Mrs. Claude Beddington, *SS,* 20. There is some disagreement about whether the nude in the canvas (*A Male Model, Seated*) described in this section is wearing a glove or not. Trevor Fairbrother, for one, sees the hand as simply being "in shadow" (email to the author, 2007).

XXXI. The quote from the "observer," *ATW*, 55. The date of D'Inverno's photograph is conjecture, though based on circumstantial evidence.

Acknowledgments

I gratefully thank the editors of the following publications in which these sections of *Tender Voyeur*, sometimes in slightly different versions, first appeared:

CIMARRON REVIEW
XXII. "Nude Study of Thomas E. McKeller"
XXVI. "Crescenzo Fusciardi"

IOWA REVIEW
IV. "Partial View of a Standing Male Nude"
XXIX. "Drag Queen"

SALMAGUNDI
I. "Boxes"
II. "Reclining Male Nude with Hands behind Head"
III. "Dream House"
V. "Bare Back"
VI. "Two Sisters"
VII. "Triple Portrait with Rhododendrons, 1985"
VIII. "Tents"
IX. "Male Head in Profile"
X. "Cigars"

SENECA REVIEW
XV. "Sonnet Excerpted from an Index of First Lines in *The Collected Poems of William Carlos Williams*"

THE SHORE
XIV. "Male Model Resting"
XVI. "Album of Figure Studies"
XVII. "Figure and Pool"

THE CLASSICAL OUTLOOK
XVIII. "Translation of Catullus's Poem 48"

I am also unspeakably grateful to both Mary Leader and Rosanne Altstatt for their close and attentive readings of *Tender Voyeur*. The book is infinitely richer for their suggestions. It has also benefited immensely on all matters of detail about Sargent's life and art from the helpful scrutiny of Trevor Fairbrother's encyclopedic eye. *Tender Voyeur*, in this lavishly illustrated edition, has been supported at every turn by Elizabeth Murphy, visionary editor of Grid Books. The book literally owes its existence to her. A million and one thanks.